Getting the money over the fence

JAMES S WITTMACK

JAMES S WITTMACK

Copyright © 2003 JAMES W WITTMACK

All rights reserved.

ISBN: **9781729314647**

DEDICATION

To all aspiring entrepreneurs and business owners that are not aware of all the different ways to get money for their business.

With the internet as a resource this book provides you with all the different types of funding that is available. To learn the intricate details of how to secure the funding utilize the internet for your specific geographic location.

CONTENTS

#		Page
1	Brief description of all the different sources of money for a business	5
2	Looking for Investor money lesson one	8
3	How to increase the odds of getting money for your company	13
4	What do lenders and investors expect you to know?	18
5	Timing for the type of money you need	22
6	Spontaneous - Temporary Funding	26
7	Understanding financials for the non-financial business owner	30
8	Ratios - a few critical ratios you must know	50
9	Loan vs need	53
10	Receivable cash strategies	56
11	Management strategies to increase cash	59
12	Cash system strategies	62
13	Cash outflow strategies	68
14	Cash leverage strategies	71
15	Term loans	74
16	Asset leverage strategies	77
17	Sell stock to get money	80
18	Sell bonds to get money	84
19	Alternative financial sources to get money	88
20	How to get money from, VC's, Investment Bankers, Angel Investors, PEG's	93
21	The DO's and DON'Ts of pitching your company	99
22	Bank CEO tells you how to get money from banks	103
23	Investment Banker tells you how to get money from alternative sources	117
24	Additional resources and reading for help	122

1 Brief Description of All the Different Sources of Funding for a Business

If you are in business you will need money at different stages;
Start-up or seed funding
Growth or expansion
Acquisition
Research and development
Project funding
IPO

The money and time you need are predetermined by your business plan.
>If you did not write a business plan you will need money (sometimes in an emergency) at unexpected times.

Make payroll
Pay Vendors
Pay legal fees
Pay accounting fees
Pay mortgage on your building

>The type of money and sources depends on your need and time you need it.

>There are different time frames money is needed for;

Seasonal
Cyclical
Long-term money
Short-term money

>There are different types of capital infusion

Loans
Investors
Stock sale

Bond Sale

There are different sources for money
Friends
Relatives
Crowdfunding
Hard money lenders who lend cash
Factoring
Banks
Bridge loans
Angel investors
PEG's – private equity groups
Venture Capitalists
Investment Bankers
Public offering

You will combine different strategies for different needs. Things you can do to get money are;
Use personal assets as collateral
Get friends or relatives to co-sign on loans
Borrow money from friends
Go to a crowdfunding site and fill out the forms
Use inventory as collateral
Use accounts receivable as collateral
Length of time in business

The strength of your financials; focus on your balance sheet and Profit and Loss
Often newer entrepreneurs wonder why a business owner would need money if their financials are strong; seasoned business owners don't wait until needing money is an emergency, they acquire it as a part of a long-term plan.

Often entrepreneurs are encouraged about how successful they are or expect they will be when money is coming in. Unfortunately, after the money starts coming in they aren't sure how to tell how much they have and whether or not they are going to have any in the future.
Entrepreneurs who discover they need money for payroll by using the O.S.W.A. (oh shucks we're out) method end up working extra hours to cover their expenses and find themselves in such a tight money crunch that they don't have time, skill or knowledge how to go to the bank or investment sources, and don't have time to learn how to utilize their financials to get out of the jam.

Working longer hours, rallying the troops and having more meetings is a temporary fix to a permanent problem. The problem will continue to surface until you put a sound money management strategy in place.

2 LOOKING FOR INVESTOR MONEY LESSON ONE

Jon and I went to the same high school together.

Both of us ended up in the business advisory industry. He specialized in hospitality and stayed on the east coast. I moved to the west coast.

Jon and one of his brothers had helped his father build his father's business into a successful chemical supply business to veterinarians.

After his father sold his business, Jon got entrenched in the fast food industry.

He eventually owned some fast food burger franchises.

He had an opportunity to build some more of the franchises on additional properties. To do that he needed some additional funding.

In Jon's search for funding, he came across an advertisement in the wall street journal. A firm was advertising they had a lot of money to lend for the right opportunities.

Jon inquired about their success rate and amount of funds they were able to secure.

Their pitch was; for a 1% due diligence fee they would take a clients opportunity to their funding sources and felt confident they could get funding for the right deals.

They were based on the west coast. They happened to be based in the same city I lived in.

GETTING THE MONEY OVER THE FENCE

Jon gave me a call and asked if he could stay at my place and if I could give him a ride to a meeting with them to secure the funding.

Jon is a CPA, MBA securities licensed professional so he is very thorough in his preparation for this type of opportunity.

He prepared a very thick business plan with all the necessary supporting data to back up his opportunity. He had included forecasts with EBITDA (earnings before interest, taxes, depreciation, and amortization), capital needs analysis and many other statistics.

They met at a business office conference room that is the type provided by corporate office rental companies. They were professionally dressed, their numbers guy asked all the right questions. The meeting seemed to go well and they felt they could get the funding in a relatively short period of time.

Jon left feeling pretty confident this was the right group that could help him. They wanted a 1% due diligence fee. Jon was looking for $3,000,000 so he needed to come up with $30,000. He felt he could get that fee reduced by providing a comprehensive package that only people in our industry understand how to prepare. They didn't agree and requested the 1% $30,000 fee to move forward.

Jon went home and started trying to find someone to fund the due diligence fee. His Dad did very well with his chemical supply company and loaned the money to Jon. Jon forwarded it to the funding group.

Three months later I got a call from Jon, he told me they felt their funding source was very strong and would come up with the money. They asked Jon if he wanted an additional $3,000,000. This was good news for Jon but there was a catch. They wanted another 1% due diligence fee. Why would they need another 1% due diligence fee if they already did the due diligence.

Jon thought this was an odd request so he asked me if I could drive by the business address they gave to him since I lived in the city they were based in. He met them at a neutral site rather than at their office for the first meeting. I drove by the location that was supposed to be their corporate office, the address was an abandoned house. I contacted Jon (this was before cell phones) and asked him to verify the address. It turned out the address was correct, the location was bogus.

Jon hired a local private investigator to verify the legitimacy of the funding group.

After 6 more weeks he had received numerous calls from the funding group saying they were about ready to give him the original $3,000,000 and needed the additional $30,000 to get the additional $3,000,000. They wanted to get the entire amount for him instead of in two payments.

While Jon's private investigator was finishing wrapping up his investigation on the group, Jon received numerous calls requesting the additional due diligence fee of $30,000.

Jon contacted me and told me he had set up another meeting with the funding group and was coming out to meet with them again. They had told him the person who was going to invest the money wanted to meet him in person. This time he was bringing his securities attorney so the legal documents could be signed if the money was made available. He said the P.I. wanted to meet with him before he went to the meeting with the funding group.

Jon and his attorney flew out and I met them at the airport. We ate at a restaurant that was close to the P.I.'s home. Afterword, we went to the P.I.'s house. He informed us the funding group was under investigation by the local undercover division of the police department. He also informed us the F.B.I. was investigating the funding group for fraud. He advised us the police department undercover division wanted to meet with us prior to the meeting and wanted our cooperation in obtaining evidence against the group.

We met with the undercover officers. They wanted one of us to wear a wire to record the meeting with the funding group. Jon's attorney was very nervous about meeting with this group after finding out they were a part of the Organized Crime Syndicate. It turns out this was one of the Organized Crime Syndicate's enterprises to scam money from business owners looking for funding.

The F.B.I. had numerous complaints against the group but didn't have any evidence to arrest or convict them.

The set up was for me to attend the initial few minutes of the meeting with Jon and his attorney and the funding group. We made up a story that I was just coming along to make sure Jon and his attorney were able to connect up with the group rather than just drop them off.

I was to identify the members and spot them as they came out of the building the meeting was in so the undercover cops could follow them.

Jon or his attorney would be the ones wearing the wire. There was no way the attorney was going to do it. He was nervous just thinking about it.

GETTING THE MONEY OVER THE FENCE

The undercover cops wired Jon's briefcase with the microphones at the latches. Jon was going to leave the briefcase locked with the latches pointing towards the Organized Crime Syndicate members.

Jon contacted the Organized Crime Syndicate group and told him he could meet around 11 a.m. This would give us enough time to stage the sting. It was a coincidence that the building the Organized Crime Syndicate wanted to meet us in was within walking distance of my condo. The 6 undercover cops, Jon, his attorney and I met at my condo two hours before the actual meeting.

The undercover cops put their cards on the kitchen counter. My wife was at work and was unaware of any of this. If she were to arrive when we were gone and seen the undercover cops cards on the counter there's no telling what would have happened.

Jon, his attorney and I walked over to the building to meet the Organized Crime Syndicate group. They had reserved a conference room on the top floor at a prestigious corporate office complex building. We all went in and introduced ourselves. I sat at the table for about 15 minutes while everyone talked small talk to get comfortable with each other.

When it was agreed they wanted to move forward with discussions regarding the funding I excused myself letting them know it wasn't necessary for me to attend that part of the meeting.

The undercover cops plan was for me to walk toward my condo and the undercover cops would pick me up to go with them and identify the Organized Crime Syndicate members as they left. After I left the meeting I walked home to the condo and no undercover cops picked me up. After getting home (keep in mind this was before cell phones) I called the undercover cops headquarters to ask where they were.

It turns out they didn't expect me to leave so soon and weren't looking for me to come out of the building so quickly.

One of the cops rushed over in his car to my condo and picked me up. They had a van parked with a large window on the side facing the building the meeting was in so I could identify any of the members as they departed. I had binoculars and was looking out the side window of the van for about an hour trying to spot someone coming out.

Eventually, I saw Jon and the attorney walking toward my condo. The undercover cops and I went back to the condo and waited for them rather than pick them up on the way. Just in case the Organized Crime Syndicate members had someone watching Jon and his attorney as they left.

Jon gave the tape of the meeting to the undercover cops who took it downtown to their headquarters. Apparently, the F.B.I. doesn't consider the undercover cops to be the same caliber as they are when it comes to this kind of thing. The undercover cops called the F.B.I. and asked them if they were looking for the Organized Crime Syndicate members. The F.B.I. confirmed they were but reiterated they didn't have any hard evidence.

The undercover cops told them they had a tape of a meeting with them. The person who had indicated he was the investor was actually the ringleader of this Organized Crime Syndicate group.

Jon and his attorney went back to the east coast. Two days later the wall street journal and my local paper announced a global sting operation where the F.B.I. had arrested 8 members of an Organized Crime Syndicate group, in Spain, England, and Germany as well as the city I lived in. The article indicated they were posing as investors, charging fees for due diligence but never attempted to get funding for the entrepreneurs.

Many entrepreneurs naively think it is a straight line to funding and they need to qualify for the investor/lender. Once they qualify they will get their money.

They often don't investigate the investor or verify their credibility. The business owner needs the money so they think the person lending it intends to give it to them if they properly qualify for the money. Unless the business owner speaks the language of the investment community they should engage the services of a seasoned professional when looking for money, especially when it is not from a highly recognized bank or investment company.

3 How to Increase the Odds of Getting Money for Your Company

When you went into business you may have thought you could survive on cash flow.

This might be true if you don't intend to grow and don't have bad surprises happen. It is critical to be prepared for the unexpected cash demands that can occur beyond your control.

Creditors won't wait until your cash flow improves.

A vendor you gave a deposit to may go out of business taking your deposit with them. Now you will need come up with the money to put a deposit down with another vendor.

Your client expects you to have the money to buy the product you need to complete their order, they aren't' going to feel they need to replace funds you lost because of your business decision of going with that vendor.

You may have received a check from a customer and used the money to make payroll, if their check doesn't clear your payroll checks bounce.

We live in a very litigate society; if you are in business you will get sued. You need money to pay your attorney and if you loose you will need to come up with the money and keep your business up and running.

Taking money out of cash flow to pay off a lawsuit is not an insurmountable task. But it leaves you with limited funds to stay in business. Money you were going to use to meet your business expenses is now gone to protect the company from legal challenges.

With proper management of your money from the start of your business you can have funds available BEFORE the problem occurs.

According to the National Association of Independent Business;

- 83% OF ALL LOANS ARE FROM BANKS

- 8% OF ALL LOANS COME FROM FINANCE COMPANIES

- 6% OF ALL LOANS COME FROM FRIENDS AND RELATIVES
- 3% OF ALL LOANS COME FROM OTHER SOURCES

Your single-most serious challenge if you are a startup business is to convince investors to invest in your enterprise. You may set up your business without investors or lenders because you may have assets you can liquidate to obtain cash. Whether or not you can launch your business with or without outside capitol, after being in business for a while, sooner or later you will require financing.

Bankers focus on the 5 c's of credit. They are most interested in, your willingness and ability to repay your obligations.

Banks are particularly concerned about your previous personal payment record. How responsible were you to pay past personal bills. They may prefer to identify collateral, your car or house on the loan.

They want collateral to back up their loan. They want to look at how you forecast your sales, profits, and evaluate the company's future potential.

Your personal involvement in every stage of the business plan is crucial when applying for a loan. The more you know about the complexities and details of every financial item in your plan; the greater the comfort level the banker will have and the better chance you have of obtaining more capital. If you have a clear understanding of the details of the financials in your business plan you can answer any question they have. If you don't know an answer it raises suspicion on their part.

Where did you get your start up funding?

Dip into savings and rely on a credit card?

If you choose to accept money from those close to you make sure you treat friends and family as you would professional lenders or stockholders. Treat the agreement in a businesslike fashion, setting everything — interest rate and other terms if it's a loan — on paper. Have the agreement in writing and pay them according to your agreement.

Angel investors often provide capital but don't get involved in running the organization. Angel investors are often retired people who like to say they invest in companies. Often they only invest 2% of their money.

Home-equity credit line, it means putting personal property at risk.

Some small business statistics to consider;
- About 28% of small companies use business credit cards
- Annual percentage rates for business credit cards with a balance carried month-to-month range from about 10% to 20%, according to a recent Bankrate.com survey.
- 39% use personal cards to finance business expenses
- Credit cards can be very expensive if you carry a balance and your interest rate is high. Still, it's one of the easiest and quickest ways to finance debt
- Average small business loans are around $30,000, occasionally as low as $10,000

Fixed overhead costs for banks make small loans a bad deal so banks prefer to loan larger amounts of money.

SBA's government-backed loans

For entrepreneurs who don't make a bank's first cut, there's the "7(a)" program. The federal agency guarantees 75% to 80% of the amount, and the lender — the bank that makes the loan — is liable for the rest. If a business receives an SBA-guaranteed loan for $5 million, the maximum guarantee to the lender will be $3,750,000 or 75%.

Because the agency will work with longer-term loans, as much as 25 years, payments are lower, allowing more businesses to qualify. But don't expect a discount; interest is at the market rate.

You may have started your business on a whim, or napkin in a restaurant. If you did you might be in the majority. Regardless of how you started your business there will come a day when you need to get money to help you through down cycles or an unexpected expense. After you have been in business for a while you need to become an excellent money manager of funds for your company. You won't always have great cash flow and you will need to do things you may not have wanted to do at the start of your company. Entrepreneurs don't realize they will need to borrow money, float liens, hedge your inventory.

When you started out you may have thought cash flow would carry you. And it did, at least for a few months or years. Business succeeds through balancing marketing and handling existing business. You get enough business to keep you busy for a while. When you do as much business as you can with them and you didn't market while handling that business then you need to market again to get more business. With adequate cash flow you can market year round and balance your incoming business.

The advantage of locating cash flow to do year round marketing is you can be more selective in the business you accept. This makes it possible for you to raise profits by raising prices. The reason you would raise prices would be to reduce sales so you could keep up with increased business because of your strong marketing program.

You need to market year round and need cash to do so. When you market year round you become a more sophisticated business professional and your market penetration strategy is in control of your business future. You are not depending on cash flow to exist.

4 WHAT DO LENDERS AND INVESTORS EXPECT YOU TO KNOW?

When an attorney appears before a judge, while the attorney is talking the judge is assessing whether or not the attorney is competent. Your investor and/or lender is expecting the same thing. So ask yourself, am I competent in the areas that will gain the confidence of the lender/investor? A competent business owner seeking funding is well prepared with answers to questions the investor/lender asks, and answers to questions they don't ask. They will be assessing the risk in lending/investing in your opportunity compared to others they have on the table. They are lending you money to get money back, your management team, market and knowledge of financials is key to their level of comfort.

If you want to put the lender/investor's mind at ease. Have a business plan that is detailed but not too long. It should be accompanied by an executive summary. In the business plan are forecast financials and existing financials if you have an existing business. If you are approaching investors you should have a pitch book and deal structure as a starting negotiating point.

WHY do you need money? YOU NEED TO KNOW THIS!

Many entrepreneurs tell me they don't want to owe anybody. They feel better if the own everything and don't owe anybody. You may find this hard to believe but lenders would be very depressed if entrepreneurs didn't want to borrow any money from them. You may be one who has had a hard time getting money and can't believe anybody wants to loan it to you. The truth; if businesses didn't borrow money, many lenders would go out of business.

The key to borrowing money is understanding;
1. What you need it for
2. How much you need
3. How long you need it for
4. How you will pay it back
5. What the lenders want
6. How to negotiate you best terms

Lenders are skeptical when a borrower drops by for some money but doesn't know the the answers to the first 4 questions.
Question one; **what do you need the money for?**

Often business owners feel they need money because payroll is difficult to meet or payables are falling behind. The reality is when you don't have money for your payroll you failed to plan ahead. You may have thought you were planning ahead. You may have thought you knew how much money was going out and coming in. This mental bookkeeping method fails to account for the complexities of a successful business.

Did you use the money for payroll to buy inventory that hasn't sold? If so, you aren't going to your lender to get money to take care of payroll you are going to them to get money to cover inventory needs.

Did you use the money you would have had for payroll to buy a new computer system? Then you need money to pay for the computer system. You need to know why you don't have money to make payroll, not just that you don't have it.

Did business slow down, and you didn't predict it? Did you keep some unproductive employees?

Be careful about keeping dedicated employees on the payroll who have been with you through thick and thin that have become unproductive. This tendency by entrepreneurs has kept many from achieving higher levels of success. The entrepreneur and employee will be better off by separating. The entrepreneur needs to maximize profits, which is the one thing they can do to provide the employees with the greatest opportunity to succeed. Without sufficient profits there is no business. The employee is better off because they can find a business that will need their knowledge.

The reality is: everyone is better off if you focus on the bottom line.

Questions 2, 3, and 4 are answered in chapter one. By analyzing your business financials you can learn how much you need, how long you need it for and how long it will take to pay it back.

Question 5; **what do lenders want?**

Lenders want to loan money that's what they do for a living. They want to know they are making a good investment and you will be able to pay them back.

Your knowledge of your financials will give them confidence in your ability to manage the money they loan to you responsibly. The strength of your financials will give them the reason to make the loan to you. They are looking for the willingness and ability to pay. Your past loan payment record will work for you if you have kept current on all loans and paid them off according to the terms stated.

Question 6; **how to negotiate the best terms for your loan?**

First and foremost is to know your financials so well you can negotiate from memory rather than having to look back and forth to determine whether or not the terms being offered are adequate for your needs. The more lenders you talk to the better ammunition you will have to negotiate on your terms.

The first 2 lenders may say no, take what you learned from them to convince the 3rd lender your business would be a good investment for them. Often if lenders find out you are looking at other choices, they will suggest you come back to them after you have talked to their competition.

Don't stop when you get a yes from the first lender that agrees to loan you money. There is no better negotiating position to be in than having the money already available when you are negotiating terms. You are in a strong negotiating position if you are able to leave the negotiations because you have a better offer.

Lenders are competing for the opportunity to loan you money. They need you and people like you to stay in business. Don't forget that.

5 TIMING FOR THE TYPE OF MONEY YOU NEED

Some entrepreneurs don't think they are big enough to have marketable securities. Putting your cash in interest bearing accounts is a prudent way to make sure you are increasing your available cash. Even the smallest companies should consider money markets, CD's, or an interest earning savings account, they may not pay much in a tight or robust economy but something is always better than nothing.

Can you get debt financing? Sell corporate bonds to fund some of your long-term needs. If you can't sell corporate bonds, you should look at getting loans.

Consider self-liquidating debt also known as a hedging principle. Self-liquidating debt is a loan to generate money to pay back the loan.

GETTING THE MONEY OVER THE FENCE

To hedge your company's liquidity means; match the money you are borrowing to the reason you are borrowing it. Don't get long-term financing for a short-term need or short-term financing for a long-term need.

Example; suppose you can cut out 2 workers salaries if you buy a piece of equipment to do their jobs. The equipment should last 15 years. Let's say the workers each earn $10,000 a year or $20,000.00 for both of them. The equipment costs $200,000.00. It will take you ten years of not paying your workers to pay for the equipment. So don't get a short-term loan or pay cash for the asset. You want to pay for it with the money you save from not paying the workers, not your cash flow or money you would need for something else.

This may be obvious to you but I can't tell you how many entrepreneurs don't think this way. They want to pay cash for everything. Then they end up without money and have difficulty getting a loan because they used up all their profits on cash purchases. Do yourself a favor; use the hedging principle when borrowing to buy assets.

Seasonal or cyclical funding. For larger companies your concern is often focused on inventory. You may need to buy more inventory in the summer so it arrives in time for the winter holiday shopping season. But the revenue from the summer sales may not be enough to pay for that inventory so you apply for a short term loan. Then repay it with the proceeds from the Holiday shopping season.

These seasonal or cyclical needs should be short-term loans. Short term loans are repaid quickly and dipped back into the next time the demand is temporary. You don't want to be borrowing money when you don't need it. If you are borrowing money just to have it you are paying interest for money you don't need.

If you need money for 12 months you don't want to borrow it for 18 months. You would end up paying interest for 6 months longer than you needed to.

For any type of equity or debt acquisition it should be clear to the entity you are getting it from what you need it for and how long you want it. They want to invest and loan money to make money for their entities. They will invest in opportunities that give them the highest return.

The lender or investor will want to grow their money. If another opportunity results in a higher return they will prefer to invest or loan to that borrower.

The amount of money isn't as important as the return they can get. Put yourself in the place of the investor or lender.

Suppose you have $10,000,000,000.00 dollars. What are your questions? Put yourself in their place.

Does this borrower have a good idea of what they need the money for? Have they demonstrated competency in handling money? Have they demonstrated the willingness to pay their debts in a timely manner?

Often entrepreneurs under estimate how much money they need thinking they have a better chance of getting less money. They think if they ask for less money they have a greater chance of getting it. This a red flag to the lender/investor. If you are not asking for enough money to stay in business they wonder how you expect to pay them back.

It's not the amount that matters, it's do you have a specific purpose for the money that makes sense.

As the investor or lender, if the risk is the same; would you rather loan $150,000 or $50,000 to a company that has the willingness and ability to pay it back at 10% interest?

You would make $15,000 on the larger loan. As long as the borrower has demonstrated competency in repaying debt and the amount is justified you would rather make $15,000 than $5,000 for the smaller loan request.

Once again, the lender or investor has whatever amount of money you need. The more they can lend or invest the better it is for them. Asking for less money than you need does not make them more willing to lend or invest in your company.

6 SPONTANEOUS - TEMPORARY FUNDING

Crowdfunding

Since 2014, all Americans can invest in emerging companies through equity crowdfunding.

There are hundreds of active investment crowdfunding deals on dozens of platforms in the United States. To see how the start/up you invested in is doing you can browse the crowdfunding platforms (Title III / Reg CF).

When crowdfunding originated anyone could offer their product or service to anyone and ask for an amount of money they wanted to get it off the ground.

Consumers were investing as little as $20 to get invested in various companies. They pay-off for them was to get a sample of the product when it was ready for market. The idea was to get a return on their investment just like an equity stock investment; as the company value increased so would their stock value.

When crowdfunding started there were no rules. Companies were offering to provide a sample of their product when they were far enough along to have one. The problem for investors was they weren't obligated to provide the product and the investor had no recourse in case it failed. At $20 a pop it didn't matter much.

Regulations were activated in May of 2016 to control crowdfunding so investors risk would be reduced.

When you are requesting a loan or investment make sure you let them know if it is for temporary or permanent needs.

TEMPORARY INVESTMENTS

Equipment, computers, printers and other assets you will sell and not replace with new equipment.

PERMANENT INVESTMENTS

If you buy an asset that lasts longer than one year it is a permanent investment.

Keep in mind the asset may have a much longer useful life than the time your company may hold on to it. Any asset you buy that sold within one year or less and not replaced is considered a temporary investment.

Spontaneous Source of Financing

You may need to come up with some money quickly. You may need to get the money from sources related to your day-to-day operations. One quick way would be to get extended credit from your suppliers.

An extremely dangerous source of money is money that is committed for another purpose.

Money set aside for taxes, payroll, and interest earned are other areas for immediate funding. This money must be paid back in a short period, make sure you do pay it back. Don't postpone paying it back for sometime in the future.

It is very easy-to-use tax money to pull yourself out of a bind and expect you will pay it back one day as soon as you can. When that big deal comes in.

A lot of taxes are payable quarterly and it is easy to be tempted to use the money for immediate cash needs, which can be relatively large and get you in a bind when you are not able to pay it back.

You must have a payback strategy in place before using the money. Businesses end up being shut down by the IRS because they keep thinking they can postpone payment until the day when the big sale or deal comes in.

Do not borrow payroll dollars that can not be repaid. Suppose you have a weekly payroll of $15,000 and you pay monthly. You have they money available until your payroll date. You may be relying on a sale that doesn't materialize.

You are personally responsible for any taxes the company can not pay back. Even if the company shuts down.

TEMPORARY SOURCES OF FINANCING

These are any sources that you can use over a period of a year. Examples of temporary sources are; current liabilities, short-term notes payable, unsecured bank loans, commercial paper, lines of credit and loans secured by accounts receivable and inventories.

PERMANENT SOURCES OF FINANCING

Loans you will need for longer than a year. Preferred stock and common stock equity are also sources for permanent financing.

GETTING THE MONEY OVER THE FENCE

7 UNDERSTANDING FINANCIALS FOR THE NON-FINANCIAL ORIENTED BUSINESS OWNER

To put your sound money management strategy in place, you **must understand 6 key financial statements.**

Once you understand how to analyze and interpret the financials you will realize a dramatic reduction in stress. You will know when and what kind of money you need to have in place to get you through cash flow down cycles in the future. You will then live a cash abundant business life with a greatly reduced financial stress level.

The six key financials are;

1. Statement of cash flows; identifies cash in and out of the company
2. Statement of retained earnings; C Corporations
3. Profit and Loss statement; tells you sales volume, expenses, net profit
4. Balance sheet; tells you how much you owe and how much you own
5. 12 month cash flow statement; tells you how much money you will need
6. Current Position; tells you how much money you have today

The first four are codependent financials; you will find data from each one of these on one or more of the others. When you combine the information from each one into a cohesive unified money management strategy you can predict when you will need money months and years ahead.

As you take a look at how they relate to each other it is easy to ascertain why you need to understand all four. The more data you have the easier it will be to zero in on the precise date you will need money and how much.

Here's how they relate to each other.

Income Statement	
Net Income	$30,000
Statement of retained earnings	
Net Income	$30,000
Ending retained earnings	$283,000
Balance Sheet	
Cash	$30,000
Stockholders equity	
Retained earnings	$283,000
Statement of cash flows	
Ending Cash	$30,000

Let's take a look at the Profit and Loss statement first. Note that the title does not have the word cash in it. You won't be able to determine how much cash you have or need from this statement. Often entrepreneurs think this statement will inform them about their cash flow.

The Profit and Loss tells you how much you have in sales, how much the products you use to make those sales cost, how much you have in expenses to make those products and get those sales, and finally how much profit or loss you have left after deducting the cost of the goods sold and expenses from the sales you made.

You deduct the loan payment to your lender and taxes you have to pay to the government for the privilege of being in business for yourself.

Even though this statement doesn't mention cash, you can use it to predict when you will need cash by determining when your sales are going to be low. When your sales are going to be low your overhead will stay the same. You will still have to pay your people and still have the cost of materials to sell, rent, phone, marketing expense, legal and accounting and the rest of your costs of being in business. When your sales are low is probably when you are going to need the money. If you can predict when your sales are going to be low you can plan ahead and have operating capital in the form that is most appropriate to fit your need. You should determine if you have a short or long term cash need.

Horizontal and vertical analyses are the most helpful when evaluating your Profit and Loss statement. When you take a look at your Profit and Loss it will be for a period of time and usually compared to another year or years for the same period of time. That's why the horizontal and vertical analysis works best for the P & L. The categories in the illustration are collapsed so you get the picture. When you compare your own P&L you will want to expand all the categories so you can see which ones need to be adjusted.

Vertical Analysis				
Income Statement	Mo. 1	%	Mo. 2	%
Sales	$50,000	100	$100,000	100
Minus - COGS	$25,000	50	$50,000	50
= Gross Profit	$25,000	50	$50,000	50
Minus - Expenses	$20,000	40	$40,000	40
= Net Profit	$5,000	10	$10,000	10
Minus - taxes/loan payment	$4,000	8	$5,000	5
= Net Profit after Taxes	$1,000	2	$5,000	5

When you compare your top to bottom numbers and percentages usually you do it from the first month of the year to the current month. For this example we are comparing the first two months of the year.

What do you see?
In this illustration there is twice as much in sales for the second month. Cost of Goods Sold are twice as much. Gross profit twice as much. Expenses twice as much.

Should expenses double? Fixed expenses wouldn't change, that is rent and items like that.

Questions you must ask yourself when analyzing your financials have to do with inconsistencies.

Because you are the business owner inconsistencies will pop out at you instantly. If you have someone else looking at them, they won't notice things you will notice.

In this illustration what caused expenses to double? You would want to look at your variable expenses, phone calls, marketing expense, expenses (variable) you have control over. Net profit doubled and net profit after taxes doubled.

It looks like the only area to be concerned about is the expense category. Ordinarily you wouldn't be concerned about that if you weren't doing a vertical analysis. The more months you compare the better you focus on ways to improve your business. Your vertical analysis is usually helpful to look at 1 month from the current year and 1 or 2 of the same months from 1 or 2 previous years. Or, 1 to 3 year annual totals next to each other.

For more than 3 periods you would look at a horizontal analysis.

Horizontal analysis of your P & L over the 1st 3 quarters of the year.

	1sr quarter	%	2nd quarter	%	3rd quarter	%
Sales	$225,000		$400,000		$80,000	
Administration	$157,500	70	$157,500	39	$157,500	197
Marketing	$22,500	10	$10,000	3	$60,000	75
Rent	$10,000	4	$10,000	3	$10,000	13
Travel Expense	$40,000	18	$33,750	8	$45,000	56
Utilities	$900	0	$600	0	$900	1
Net Profit	$4,100	2	$198,150	50	($183,000)	(229)

Horizontal (left to right) analysis. What do you see in this illustration that doesn't look correct? The third quarter shows negative numbers. An entrepreneur who doesn't do horizontal analysis might panic and think they have to close the business.

As you can see, your sales might be directly affected by your marketing dollars which take 3 to 6 months before results show up on your financials.

Do you consider marketing dollars, money invested? or money spent? If you look at marketing as an expense you would probably consider cutting back on the money you spend in marketing. If you look at marketing as an investment, you would probably consider making sure you invest wisely.

In this illustration when you invested more marketing dollars in the 1st quarter, it paid off in the second quarter. You invest less in the 2nd quarter and it may have blown your 3rd quarter potential.

You will also find is the way the percentages change relative to the numbers. You were able to keep administration under control each month, because of the sales revenues administration changed in percentage even though the numbers stayed the same.

Travel expense also was higher in the 1st quarter which may have contributed to the higher sales in the 2nd quarter. This entrepreneur may have been thinking that they could cut back on traveling and investing in marketing and get the same sales. Possibly after the 1st month of the 3rd quarter they realized they needed to invest more in marketing and travel more to get sales up.

The problem is they may have realized this a little late. Now they have a huge negative to make up in the fourth quarter. All they can do is hope it will turn around.

This is typical of an entrepreneur who is not analyzing their financials. They are reacting too late, by the time they figure out the solution so much time has passed it becomes a crisis management situation, reacting rather than being proactive. Some entrepreneurs pride themselves in not spending money. They focus on things like utilities and phone bills rather than the big picture.

Saving money in the wrong places loses sales. If this entrepreneur did not plan ahead they probably don't have the money to cover their payroll for the 3rd quarter. If they planned ahead they acquired appropriate funding to get them through the 3rd quarter. How did they do in the 4th quarter?

Comparing P & L Expenses vs Sales Amounts

	1st Qtr	%	2nd Qtr	%	3rd Qtr	%	4th Qtr	%
Sales	$225,000		$400,000		$80,000		$600,000	
Marketing	$157,500	70	$157,500	39	$157,500	197	$187,500	31
Travel	$10,000	4	$10,000	3	$10,000	75	$30,000	5
Total Expense	$40,000	18	$33,750	8	$45,000	56	$33,750	6
Utilities	$900	0	$600	0	$900	1	$900	0
Net Profit	$4,100	2	$198,150	50	($183,400)	(-229)	$347,850	58

According to this illustration it looks like the investment, in marketing paid off. It also looks like the traveling is necessary. If you are looking at your financials a month at a time instead of over a year you might get scared in the 3rd quarter.

You also can tell you need to borrow money in the 2nd Quarter (line of credit) to cover your 3rd quarter lack of sales. You then re-pay the (line of credit) in the 4th quarter.

Many entrepreneurs look at marketing as an immediate return category. The reality is, marketing is a long term investment, to put a marketing plan together takes months, during this time the money is going out for it, the money that comes back is not until the following months and years.

It looks like almost all the money made in the first 2 quarters was lost in the 3 quarter. When you look at the 4th quarter it looks like the money was well spent. The type of loan that would be good for this 3rd quarter problem is probably a line of credit. A line of credit is short term and can get you through a bump in the road when sales are slow that is repaid when sales are high. The money can be paid back in the 4th quarter.

The more time you can compare your months or years of financials the more clear a pattern surfaces which improves the accuracy of your decisions. 2 or more years are very helpful, more is better. This entrepreneur may find every year the 3rd quarter is low or it is a matter of how they invest their marketing money. Often it is a combination.

Look at the 1st quarter down by month.
Horizontal Analysis – 1st quarter

Income Statement	Month 1	Month 2	Month 3
Sales	$50,000	$100,000	$75,000
Minus - COGS	$25,000	$50,000	$37,500
= Gross Profit	$25,000	$50,000	$37,500
Minus - Expenses	$20,500	$42,000	$32,000
= Net Profit	$4,500	$8,000	$4,600
taxes/loan payment	$4,000	$5,000	$4,000
= Net Profit after Taxes	$500	$3,000	$600

Sales doubled in the 2nd month over the 1st month, and dropped down to 1 ½ higher in the third month than the 1st month. How come net profit didn't double in the 2nd month? What about the third month? That is even worse, net profit was only higher by $100. It shows up in the net profit in the same way.

It has to be somewhere in expenses. It looks like it would be a good idea to ask for the expanded detail version of your P & L for these three months.

You would have the numbers person compare all 3 months on the same page and have them include percentages. The percentage variance will pop out at you, and then you can zero on the dollar amount that seems out of whack. When you figure out what expense or expenses are of concern, get a detailed expanded spreadsheet on that category. It could be a check entered for the wrong amount and possibly entered in the wrong month.

A good way to see how you are doing is by having the numbers shown to you in graphic form.

Horizontal Analysis in a picture

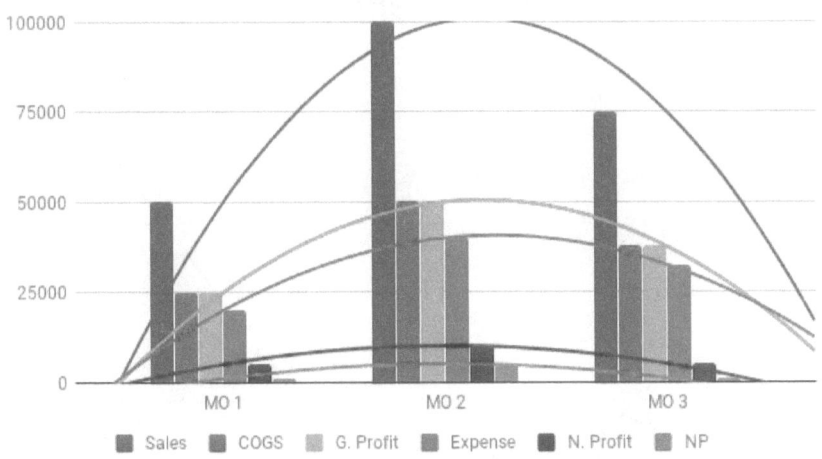

This bar chart is a good indicator of areas to look at to improve. Right away you see areas you need to improve. It helps to look at it in picture form first and then look at the details of the breakdown on the spreadsheet to confirm your suspicions.

The above chart is for multiple categories, the following chart will examine 1 category so you can zero in on ways to improve that specific area of your financials. For this hypothetical illustration I have chosen to evaluate sales for the last 3 years.

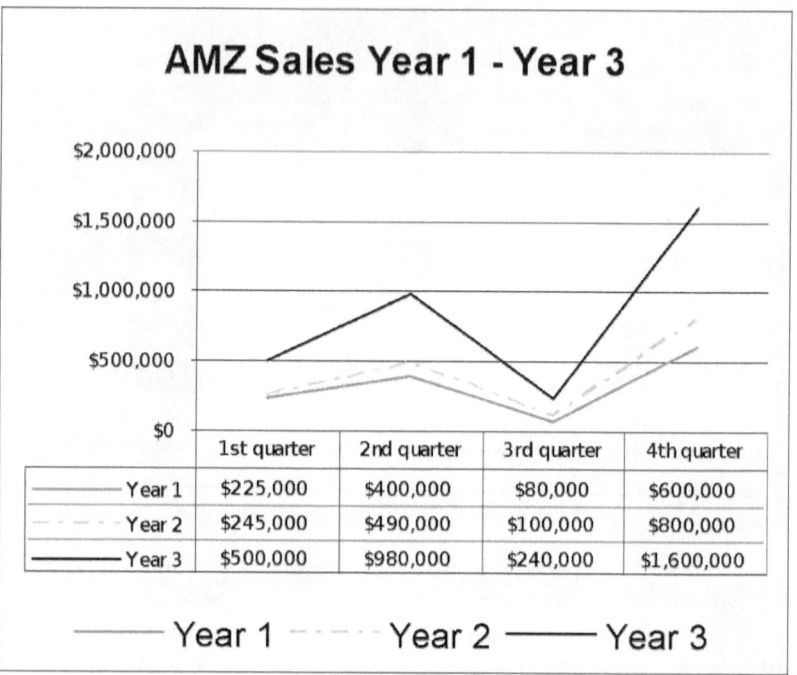

Looks like you've learned something about your 1st quarter that will be of tremendous benefit. The 3rd quarter needs the same kind of attention. You did more than double in year three in the 3rd quarter, which is a good sign. It seems to stay in the worst revenue producing part of your year. Can you have a parking lot sale? Possibly some specials on your web site would help. Can you have a sale earlier in the year or would that take away from your fourth quarter sales?

You can be proud of your accomplishments for the 1st and 2nd years. It looks like they are paying off in your third year.

Statement of retained earnings analysis.

C corporation. A C corporation is not taxed on money it keeps to reinvest in the company. After paying its bills and debts and distributing **profits** to shareholders and owners, the **C corporation** can invest the remaining funds in the company. This reinvested amount is a type of equity called **retained earnings**. You can interchange the words "retained earnings" with the words "money you keep". Retained earnings can be kept in a separate account and are tax-exempt until they are distributed as salary, dividends, or bonuses. The following table is a comparison of two years.

S corporation. S corps can distribute profits to their shareholders, keep them as retained earnings or do a little of both. The difference is that the regular corporation makes this decision after it pays corporate income taxes. An S corp doesn't pay taxes. The shareholders pay all the taxes on the company's profit, no matter what the company does with that profit.

Retained Earnings	End of 2nd Year	End of 1st Year
Beginning Balance	$366,700	$.00
Net Income	$100,000	$336,700
Cash Dividends Paid	$.00	$.00
Treasury Stock Issued	$.00	$.00
Ending Balance	$376,700	$366,700

You will want to consider your legal structure when determining whether or not to keep your retained earnings in the business or take them out as a bonus. The tax consequences may be the determining factor in whether or not you keep or distribute the retained earnings. It may be cheaper to pay taxes on the money as a bonus to yourself than for the company to pay taxes on it and you pay taxes on it after distribution.

<u>Statement of cash flows</u>

This statement helps you learn where you are using your cash.

Statement of Cash Flow

Cash flow from operating activities	Year 2	Year 1
Net cash flows from operating activities	$55,000	$25,000
Cash flows from investing activities		
Net cash flows from investing	$100,000	($20,000)
Cash Flows from financing Activities		
Net cash flows used for financing	($150,000)	$.00
Net increase (decrease) in cash	$5,000	$5,000
Beginning Cash	$10,000	$5,000
Ending Cash	**$15,000**	**$10,000**

The analysis of the statement of cash flows tells you where you are getting your cash and whether or not you are doing a good job using it. Let's take a look at an analysis of the above statement of cash flows and see how this entrepreneur is doing.

Analysis of Cash Flow

Operating Activities		
Income from Operations		$40,000
Add (subtract) non-cash items		
Depreciation	$15,000	
Net increase in current assets other than cash	-$5000	
Net increase in current liabilities	$5,000	$15,000
Net cash inflow from operating activities		**$55,000**
Investing Activities		
Sale of property, plant, and equipment	$100,000	
Net cash inflow from investing activities		**$100,000**
Financing Activities		
Issuenace of bonds payable	$75,000	
Payment of long-term debt	($200,000)	
Purcahse of treasury stock	($5,000)	
Payment of Dividends	($20,000)	
Net cash outlfow from financing activities		($150,000)
Increase in cash		**$5,000**

What do you think? Looks like we've got some problems here doesn't it? Matter of fact, it looks like the companies going bankrupt. Why? They sold a lot of equipment they used to make their product to get cash. They got cash but where are they going to get the money to get new equipment to replace the equipment sold? Their running out of cash quickly aren't' they?

Where would you start to look for solutions? You'll find that in the management techniques section of this book. There are many solutions, the question is; is there enough time to learn these financials while you are still trying to make payroll? The answer is: you <u>must make the time</u>.

The balance sheet

Money or liquidity for running your business is generally called working capital. If you deposit your companies' checks at night and pay the payroll you are handling the liquidity of your company. How do you know how much working capital you have? Working capital is determined by subtracting current liabilities (found on the balance sheet, not all liabilities, just current liabilities) from current assets (off the balance sheet). Current assets are not just cash.

Current assets are everything you can turn into cash within a year;
1. Cash
2. Marketable securities
3. Accounts receivable, and inventories.

Many companies' current assets are equal to or more that half of all the assets for the company. Your balance sheet tells you how much you owe and how much you own. The significant difference from this statement and the others is the balance sheet can be evaluated at a specific point in time. The other statements are for a period of time. You might want to know how much you own and how much you owe today. You would use your balance sheet to find the answers.

Balance Sheet

	Year 2	Year 1
Assets		
Total current assets	$355,000	$115,000
Net property, plant, equipment	$113,000	$121,000
Net Intangibles	$5,000	$2,000
Total Assets **(what you OWN)**	$473,000	$238,000
Liabilities and Shareholder Investment		
Total Current liabilities	$195,500	$38,500
Total shareholder investment	$270,000	$196,000
Total liabilities **(what you OWE)**	$473,000	$238,000

Let's take a look at how you are doing compared to your industry. Because you are looking at percentages the dollar amount of the comparison doesn't matter.

It looks like the area to focus on is in the receivables and long term assets. You have less in long term assets than your industry. Your receivables are higher than the industry average. Are customers paying late? Are you letting too many customers have credit?

Let's see how you are doing compared to another company. You can get the data on a public company in your industry off the internet. Your closest competitor's data may not be available if they are a private company and a public company's data will be fine.

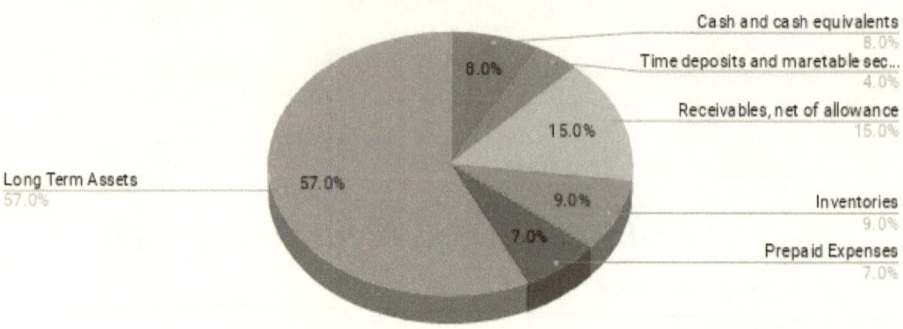

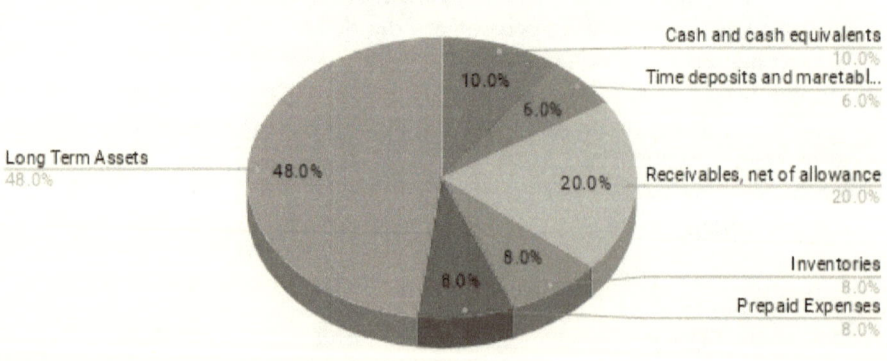

Because these are comparisons of percentages not dollars it doesn't matter how big the company is you are comparing. This is helpful because it helps you learn know how you are doing relative to another company. If you only look at your data it limits your ability to judge the level of your success.

By knowing how to analyze your financials you can determine when you will need money and how much. Determine if you need long term or short term money and go get it.

GETTING THE MONEY OVER THE FENCE

Your company percentages

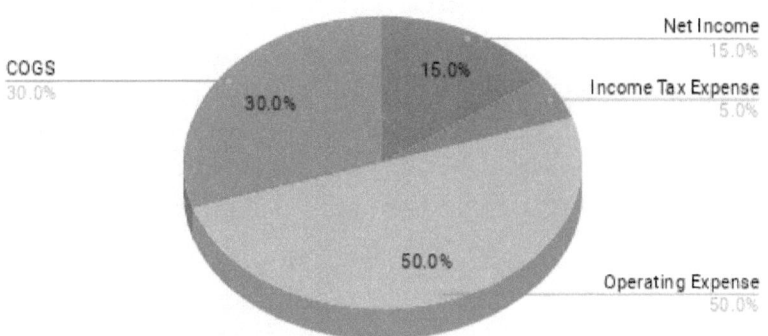

Your industry percentages

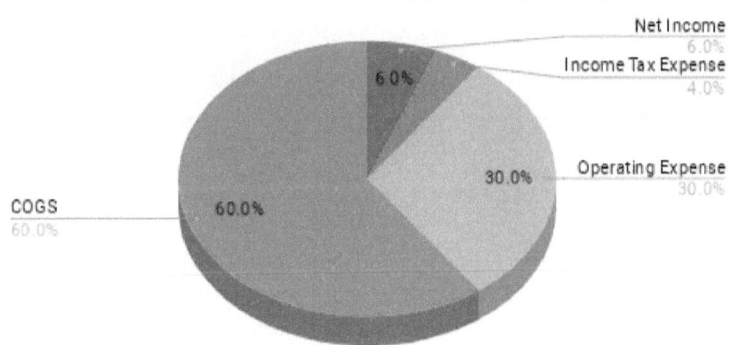

JAMES S WITTMACK

12 month cash flow forecast

Twelve-month cash flow	Pre-Startup EST	1	2	3	4	5	6	7	8	9	10	11	12	Comany Name		Fiscal Year Begins: 2005 Total Item EST
Cash on Hand (beginning of month)		0	-9,263	-18,607	-30,996	-63,080	-107,580	-90,008	-63,264	-14,960	-6,649	3,971	16,514			
CASH RECEIPTS																
Cash Sales		73,125	146,250	146,250	146,250	146,250	292,500	292,500	292,500	292,500	292,500	292,500	292,500			2,705,625
Collections fm CR accounts																
Loan/ other cash in	350,000															
TOTAL CASH RECEIPTS	350,000	73,125	146,250	146,250	146,250	146,250	292,500	292,500	292,500	292,500	292,500	292,500	292,500			2,705,625
Total Cash Available (before cash out)	350,000	73,125	136,987	127,643	107,254	83,167	184,917	212,492	249,216	277,507	285,852	296,471	309,014			2,705,625
CASH PAID OUT																
Purchases (merchandise)																
Purchases (specify)																
Purchases (specify)																
Outsoucing Valuations		13,750	27,500	27,500	27,500	27,500	18,500	17,500	17,500	14,500	14,500	14,500	14,500			235,250
Payroll expenses (taxes, etc.)	33,750	61,270	91,005	111,133	114,486	126,196	156,094	202,599	211,006	229,705	229,705	229,705	229,705			2,025,600
Professional Expenses																
Supplies (office & oper)	500	100	100	100	100	100	700	200	200	800	300	300	300			3,300
Repairs & maintenance																
Marketing and Sales	5,000	2,650	2,650	2,650	2,650	2,050	2,250	2,250	2,250	2,350	2,350	2,350	1,550			29,000
Accounting & legal	5,000	2,000	2,000	2,000	2,000	2,000	2,000	2,000	2,000	2,000	2,000	2,000	2,000			24,000
Rent	0	0	19,056	9,878	9,878	19,056	14,466	14,466	14,466	14,716	14,716	14,716	14,716			160,130
Telephone	1,500	1,500	1,500	1,500	1,500	1,500	3,000	3,000	3,000	3,000	3,000	3,000	3,000			29,500
Utilities	0	500	500	500	500	500	2,000	1,000	1,000	2,000	1,500	1,500	1,500			13,000
Insurance	300	300	300	300	300	300	300	300	300	300	300	300	300			3,600
Vehicle Expense	425	1,200	1,600	1,600	1,600	1,600	2,000	2,000	2,000	2,000	2,000	2,000	2,000			21,600
Travel Analysis & Valuation	600	3,100	3,100	3,100	3,100	3,100	3,100	3,100	3,100	3,100	3,100	3,100	3,100			37,200
Traveling Mgrs	500	300	500	500	1,000	1,000	1,000	1,000	1,000	1,000	1,000	1,000	1,000			10,300
Travel Intis Systems	1,450	450	450	450	450	450	2,650	650	650	2,650	1,450	300	300			10,900
Internet	46	46	46	46	46	56	56	92	92	92	126	126	126			1,078
Postage	100	125	125	125	125	125	250	250	250	375	375	375	275			2,875
Miscellaneous	100	100	100	100	100	100	0	200	200	300	300	300	300			2,100
SUBTOTAL	49,271	77,391	150,532	161,472	165,345	185,633	249,362	250,607	259,014	279,034	276,724	275,584	274,784			2,605,221
Loan principal payment		5,016	5,042	5,067	5,092	5,118	5,143	5,168	5,195	5,221	5,247	5,273	5,299			61,881
Capital purchase cost per office	127,170						10,480									
Other startup costs																
Reserve and/or Escrow																
Owners Withdrawal																

This is a very critical report that reveals how much cash you will need and when you will need it. Below you will see the cash position row copied from this illustration in larger font for easier reading. You will see the 10th month is the 1st month the company is cash positive. It tells you/your investors/lenders when you will have money to pay them back in addition to when you will have positive cash flow to run your company.

GETTING THE MONEY OVER THE FENCE

On the following page you will see the cash available at the end of each month first 5 months on the first line and the last 7 months on the second line.

The company starts out with a negative of -$9,282.91 in the first month, and continues to be negative through month 9. Month 10 is the first cash positive month. This tells you and your investor/lender you will begin to be able to start paying them back after month 10. When you start to have cash positive months you continue the forecast with the loan or debt payment back to them showing them you will continue to be able to pay them. This should be forecast for at least another year. In some cases the lender/investor may want you to forecast it until they are paid back in full.

If you are not borrowing money and using your own money this will tell you when you will begin to be able to pay yourself back. This is why this report is so critical. It will help reduce an immense amount of cash stress pressure knowing when you will have cash.

You must adjust this to actual numbers each month to compare actual cash flow to projected. You may have money before you projected having it. You may also find you may have to make some adjustments because it will take longer than projected to realize positive cash flow. This only concerns investors/lenders if you don't keep track of the cash flow.

	Pre-Startup EST	1	2	3	4	5
Cash Position (end of month)	$173,559.00	-$9,282.91	$18,606.90	-$38,895.60	-$63,082.63	-$107,583.12

6	7	8	9	10	11	12	Total Item EST
-$80,008.25	-$43,284.09	-$14,993.28	-$6,647.93	$3,871.32	$15,514.34	$27,930.99	$38,410.99

The following "current position" report should be prepared every monday morning until you are comfortable and understand how much cash you have well enough to rely on the report once a month.

JAMES S WITTMACK

The information for this report comes from your other financial reports and bank statements.

CURRENT POSITION

1. **Cash On Hand** (including Petty Cash)			24,392
2. Marketable **Securities** / Avail. **Line of Credit**			5,000
3. Other **Investments**			
4. **Misc**ellaneous Receivables	(Misc. Employee Loans)		
5. **Accounts Receivable**	Current	37%	3,648
	30 Days	30%	2,977
	60 Days	0%	13
TOTAL A/R $9.919	90 Days	33%	3,281
	Over 90 Days	0%	0
6. **Notes Receivable**	Current		0
	Long Term		0
7. **Inventory**	Finished Goods	0%	0
TOTAL INV: 426,394	Work In Process	0%	0
	Mat'l & Supplies	0%	0
8. **Real Estate**	Land		____
	Building		____
9. **Machinery** and **Equipment**, NET VALUE			0
10. **Furniture** and **Fixtures**, NET VALUE			31,401
11. **Accounts Payable**	Current	44%	12,197
	30 Days	7%	2,028
TOTAL A/P: 27,580	60 Days	0%	115
	90 Days	48%	13,240
	Over 90 Days	0%	
12. Notes Payable	Total Debt		942,835
	Monthly Debt Service		
13. Monthly **Rental** Payments (or Mortgage)			7,170

	PROPERTY	PAYROLL	SALES	TOTAL TAXES
14. **Taxes** Payable	____	____	2,009	2,009 2,009
15. **Weekly Cash** Receipts (see Table, below)				12,359
16. Sales **Backlog**				
17. Weekly **Payroll** NET 12,000 GROSS 15,000				15,000

Projected Ann
Vol.@52xAv.Wkly
642,674
CALCULATION
S

TABLE: Deposit Analysis for Weekly Receipts Determination

GETTING THE MONEY OVER THE FENCE

Deposits: Most Recent			Deposit Should	Be Entered On Line	
Date	Amount		Date	Amount:	
1. 5/29/2008	1,285	7.	5/20/2008	617	Total
Deposits					
2. 5/28/2008	2,180	8.	5/19/2008	9,501	
30,015.00					
3. 5/27/2008	3,715	9.	5/16/2008	1,246	Total Days 1st-
Last					
4. 5/23/2008	4,435	10.	5/15/2008	874	<u>17</u>
5. 5/22/2008	372	11.	5/14/2008	3,750	=Deposits/Day
6. 5/21/2008	658	12.	5/13/2008	1,382	<u>1,765.59</u>
					Av. Wkly
Receipts					
					<u>12,359.12</u>

I have reviewed the last (3) months bank statement and found the following:
Number of checks returned for Non-Sufficient Funds   2
Number of checks that had payment Stopped   0

    This is a very brief overview of the financials. Once you have your financials printed and start analyzing them you will discover many ways to improve your cash flow.

    Once you start to understand your financials your decisions about your business will be based on fact and you will find you make much better decisions and have a lot less stress.

    By being in control of your financials you will eliminate crisis management and fires to put out, and business will be fun again.

8 RATIOS - A FEW CRITICAL RATIOS YOU MUST KNOW

These ratios are a few of the most important ratios to understand when analyzing your financials. Understanding ratios is as important and in some cases more important than understanding the financials. From the ability to pay current liabilities to how successful your company is at earning a profit.

is = data from income statement **bs** = data from balance sheet **div** = divide

CURRENT RATIO Measures ability to pay current liabilities with current assets, a higher current ratio indicates a stronger financial position. It suggest a business has sufficient liquid assets to maintain normal business operations

Measuring the companies ability to pay current liabilities
working capital = current assets - current liabilities

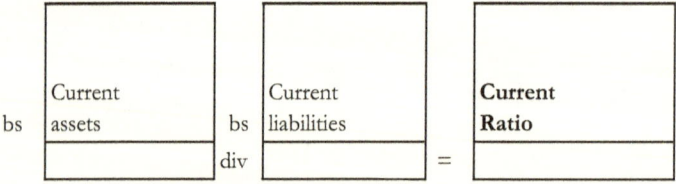

ACID TEST RATIO shows ability to pay all current liabilities if they come due immediately, to do so the company would have to convert most liquid assets to cash. From your balance sheet.

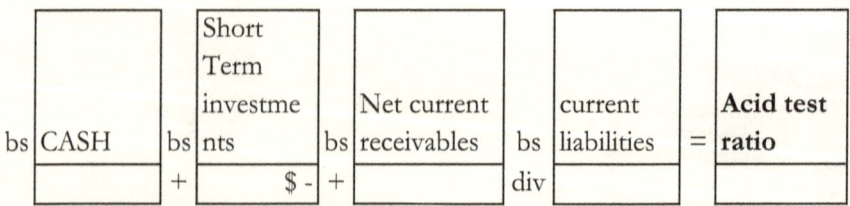

ACCOUNTS RECEIVABLE TURNOVER Measure ability to collect cash

from credit customers, in general the higher the ratio the more successfully the business collects cash, and the better off its operations are. If receivable turnover is too high it may indicate that credit is too tight, causing the loss of sales to good customers

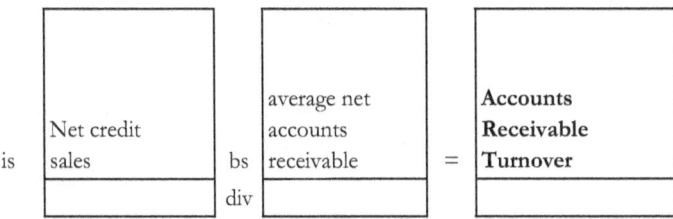

DAY'S SALES IN RECEIVABLES Shows how many days sales remain in Accounts Receivable-how many days it takes to collect the average level of receivables, the lower the accounts receivable balance, the more successful the business has been in converting receivables into cash, the better off the business.

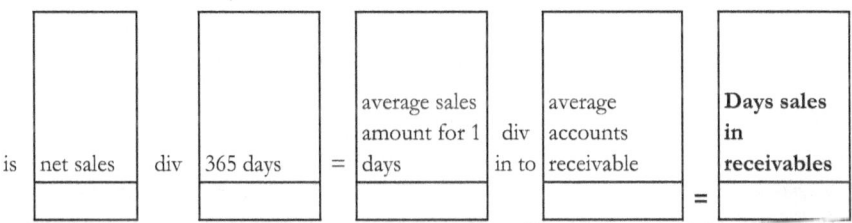

DEBT RATIO Indicates percentage of assets financed with debt, the higher the debt ratio the higher the strain of paying interest each year and principal amount at maturity. Creditors generally charge higher interest rates on new borrowing to companies with an already high debt ratio

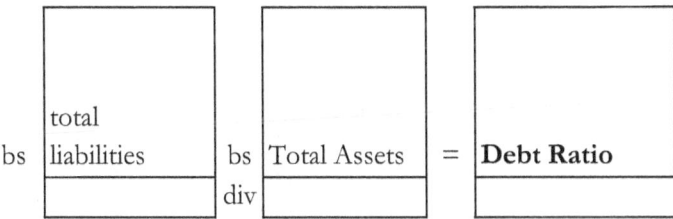

TIMES INTEREST EARNED RATIO Measures the number of times operating income can cover interest expense, it's also called the interest coverage ratio. A high times interest earned ratio indicates ease in paying

interest expense; a low value suggests difficulty

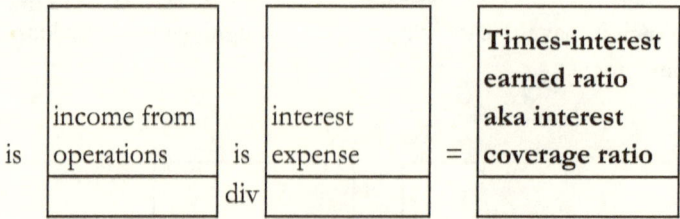

RATE OF RETURN ON SALES also called return on sales. This shows the percentage of each sales dollar earned as net income. A high rate of return is best. The higher the rate the more net sales dollars are providing income to the business and the fewer net sales dollars are absorbed by expenses.

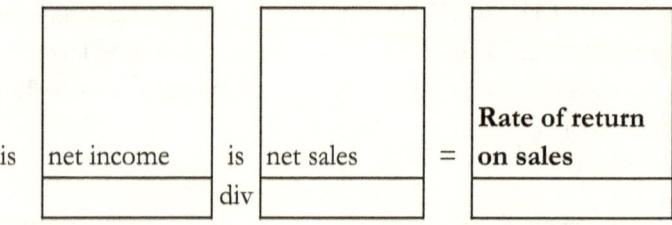

RATE OF RETURN ON ASSETS also called return on assets, measures a company's success in using its assets to earn a profit. creditors have loaned money to the company, and the interest they receive is the return on their investment. Net income is the stockholders return. Net income and interest expense are taken from the income statement, the average beginning and ending total assets from the balance sheet.

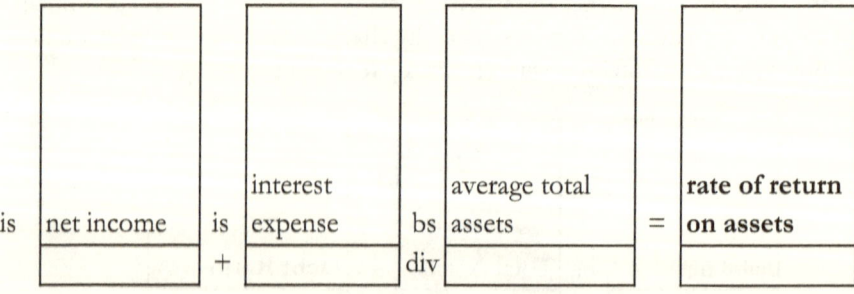

9 LOAN VS NEED

The type of loan you need is determined by the need you have for the loan. You don't need a long term loan to get you through the holiday season. You don't want a short term loan to buy equipment that lasts 20 years.

Short Term Credit
Unsecured loans
    The lender trusts the borrower to pay it back. A business that has been in existence for a long time applies for this loan.
    Sources;
- Accrued wages
- Accrued taxes
- Trade Credit
- Unsecured bank loans
- Commercial paper

    Line of credit:

Source; Commercial Bank
    A line of credit is an informal agreement with your bank that allows you to use up to a given amount to cover your cash flow ebbs and tides. The bank does not have to give the line of credit for your company even after you have arranged for the line to be available for your use. The line of credit is

based on the financials for a company's' fiscal year. You pay a variable interest rate based on the prime rate at the bank. Prime rate is the rate the major banks can loan money to smaller banks based on the rate the major banks pay the government. You can see if you can get the bank to negotiate a lower rate if you have had favorable borrowing success with them in the past. In most cases the borrower keeps a <u>minimum balance</u> at the bank while using the line of credit. This the <u>compensating balance</u>.

Transaction loans
Commercial banks

A transaction loan is for a specific purpose. You need to sign a promissory note as collateral. The promissory note is similar to a line of credit regarding cost, term, maturity and compensating balance needs. In both cases the lender likes a zero balance to during the year. The reason banks want to achieve the short-term zero balance is to make sure the promissory note is not used for short-term financing.

Commercial Paper

Commercial paper is a short-term promise to pay in the debt market. The company or a dealer sells it. Company direct placements of commercial paper is four times greater than through a commercial paper dealer. You know the story the rich get richer? This is a similar situation; the bigger more credit worth the company the bigger they can get by getting more favorable loans. Only the largest companies with the best credit can get commercial paper.

Commercial paper debt is paid in 9 months or less, most in less than 6 months. Commercial paper is a low interest rate. Lower than the prime rate banks pay for their loans.

Benefits

1. Lower interest rates than bank loans
2. No minimum balance requirement
3. Offers large amounts of credit

Unsecured credit payment terms
Sources

Early payment discount; often you may take an extra discount if paid early. Pay it early and TAKE IT.

Pay late; If you find your company in this situation, you should consider approaching an institution sooner rather than later for a loan. Late payments make it more difficult to get a loan. When in a tight cash flow crunch you may need to forgo the discount and extend the payment to a later date. For instance suppose your terms are 60 days. You may need to extend your payment until 80 days. Be careful here, the credit terms offered are cancelled if you abuse their policy too often.

Secured loans

The lender is uncomfortable lending the money without some kind of guarantee from the borrower. Requires specific assets to be available for liquidation by the lender if the borrower does not pay as promised.

Sources
1. Commercial banks
2. Finance Companies
3. Factors

10 RECEIVABLE CASH STRATEGIES

Short Term Credit
Unsecured loans
  The lender trusts the borrower to pay it back. A business that has been in existence for a long time applies for this loan.
  Sources;
- Accrued wages
- Accrued taxes
- Trade Credit
- Unsecured bank loans
- Commercial paper
  Line of credit:

Source; Commercial Bank
  A line of credit is an informal agreement with your bank that allows you to use up to a given amount to cover your cash flow ebbs and tides. The

bank does not have to give the line of credit for your company even after you have arranged for the line to be available for your use. The line of credit is based on the financials for a company's' fiscal year. You pay a variable interest rate based on the prime rate at the bank. Prime rate is the rate the major banks can loan money to smaller banks based on the rate the major banks pay the government. You can see if you can get the bank to negotiate a lower rate if you have had favorable borrowing success with them in the past. In most cases the borrower keeps a <u>minimum balance</u> at the bank while using the line of credit. This the <u>compensating balance</u>.

Transaction loans
Commercial banks

A transaction loan is for a specific purpose. You need to sign a promissory note as collateral. The promissory note is similar to a line of credit regarding cost, term, maturity and compensating balance needs. In both cases the lender likes a zero balance to during the year. The reason banks want to achieve the short-term zero balance is to make sure the promissory note is not used for short-term financing.

Commercial Paper

Commercial paper is a short-term promise to pay in the debt market. The company or a dealer sells it. Company direct placements of commercial paper is four times greater than through a commercial paper dealer. You know the story the rich get richer? This is a similar situation; the bigger more credit worth the company the bigger they can get by getting more favorable loans. Only the largest companies with the best credit can get commercial paper.

Commercial paper debt is paid in 9 months or less, most in less than 6 months. Commercial paper is a low interest rate. Lower than the prime rate banks pay for their loans.

Benefits

1. Lower interest rates than bank loans
2. No minimum balance requirement
3. Offers large amounts of credit

Unsecured credit payment terms
Sources

Early payment discount; often you may take an extra discount if paid early. Pay it early and TAKE IT.

Pay late; If you find your company in this situation, you should consider approaching an institution sooner rather than later for a loan. Late payments make it more difficult to get a loan. When in a tight cash flow crunch you may need to forgo the discount and extend the payment to a later date. For instance suppose your terms are 60 days. You may need to extend your payment until 80 days. Be careful here, the credit terms offered are cancelled if you abuse their policy too often.

Secured loans

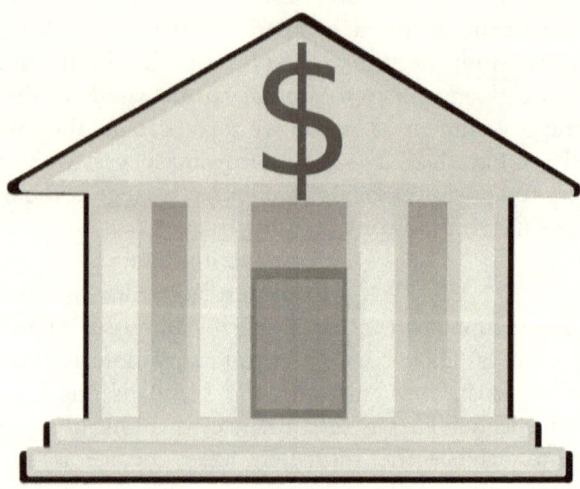

The lender is uncomfortable lending the money without some kind of guarantee from the borrower. Requires specific assets to be available for liquidation by the lender if the borrower does not pay as promised.

Sources
1. Commercial banks
2. Finance Companies
3. Factors

11 MANAGEMENT STRATEGIES TO INCREASE CASH

When some business owners think of managing their money for their business, they think it means not spending it. This may work for a family budget but not for a business.

Managing money for your business means SPENDING IT WISELY. Spending it means you need to know when you will need it before it runs out. You need to know what you will use it for. You don't want to spend your cash on something that can wait until you increase sales to get more cash.

Some business owners feel they don't want to increase their marketing expense. These same business owners want increased sales. How do you increase sales without marketing? Why does the most recognized name in the world, (coca cola) continue to advertise spending millions of dollars a year on advertising?

Marketing is **investing** in your company. Think of marketing as an investment not an expense section of your financials. If the business owner who feels managing the money for their business means not spending it were in charge of coca cola, the company would have filed for bankruptcy years ago.

Tight management of accounts receivable and inventory

The typical company has about 25% of its total assets in accounts receivable. Managing these accounts is without question a critical part of being a sound company. Three factors affect the size of your accounts receivable;
- Percentage of credit sales to total sales

- Level of sales
- Credit and collection policies of your firm

The longer an account goes uncollected the harder it is to get the money and the higher the probability you won't get paid. You want to keep the accounts as current as possible to avoid the obvious problems with stringing out payment.

Identify accounts that are getting behind and try to collect them.
Methods of collection are;
- Past due letter
- Telephone call
- Stronger letter
- Collection agency

You need to test the viability of the account. It goes without saying, an account that doesn't pay is not a good account. It is even a bigger problem if they buy a lot and don't pay.

You need to take a detailed look at how you are handling your accounts receivable and inventory. Make sure you're collecting your past due fees and getting your invoices out. One approach to this is to take away a discount if offered if the invoice isn't paid within your terms. For example; if you are charging 2% past due fees, you collect 2% for late payments. Suppose you offer 10% to 50% off the retail price to your customer, if they don't pay within the given time frame they don't get the discount, they have to pay full price. If you have accounts, you can't afford to keep use this method. Once an account is required to pay full price when they thought they were getting a discount they may went elsewhere for their supplies. Make sure it is an account you don't mind losing.

Make sure your inventory is not out of balance. Check the inventory turns of your industry to your inventory turns. It is a little tricky because high turns may mean you don't carry enough inventory and could lose customers low inventory could mean you are carrying too much inventory. Every item needs to be checked for how it is merchandised at your customer's location and how you are promoting it. If you have too much inventory offer discounts to get rid of it. If you have too little, you may consider raising prices to slow down the purchasing. This is an interesting tactic because sometimes you learn you could sell at higher margins and got caught up in discounting so much you lost your focus on profitability.

Just in time production, inventory, and delivery (JIT)

GETTING THE MONEY OVER THE FENCE

This is a production management and inventory control system. It cuts inventory down to a minimum and it cuts the distance between production operations. You may find costs of establishing close relationships with your suppliers may rise somewhat. The tradeoff is the speed you can get new inventory supplied. This allows you to maintain a lower inventory level with the obvious positive ramifications. Taiichi Okno, one of the Toyota Vice Presidents, originated it in Japan.

The concept is for suppliers to provide parts as needed rather buying a lot of inventory and using it up and re-ordering. These parts would be available "Just In Time", the "JIT" system. Many companies have a comfort level of carrying massive inventories, "Just In Case" they need them. If interest rates are high having inventory on hand, you don't use right away could be a very costly way to keep inventory. If rates are low, it makes a little more sense, but still doesn't have the advantages of "JIT". Consider the distance between you and your supplier, your facility needs to handle a much higher frequency of delivery so you need more dock doors, you need less space. This is something you need to consider in your strategic plan.

Tight management of payables

The other side of the receivables coin is your ability to get extended terms from your suppliers. You want to get your money fast and pay it out slow. Why? Put the money into an interest bearing account and let it grow.

12 Cash system strategies

Cash management
What is the cash in your business?

It's the currency and coins in your cash drawers, registers or checking accounts.

Near cash is the marketable securities that can be converted into cash. A security in this category can be liquidated in a year or less. Together these are your liquid assets.

Your goal is to always pay your liabilities on time. If you can't you may find the term insolvency used during discussions of your firm by creditors. You need to avoid this predicament.

Carry enough amounts of cash to pay your bills, don't tie up too much money for this purpose, but set aside the right amount. If you have too much money in cash it diminishes your profitability, which affects your ability to get credit.

Focus;
- Speed up cash collections and slow or control cash outflows
- Put the cash in marketable securities whenever suitable for increase your returns

1. Speed up **cash coming in**
   a. **Mail Float;** the time between when a customer mails their payment and the time you get it to your bank.
   b. **Processing Float;** the time between when you get the check and it gets into your bank account.
   c. **Transit Float;** this is how long it takes for the check to clear and be usable in your account.
   d. **Disbursing Float:** the money that's available to you until the check you write to your supplier clears your supplier's account.

You may think not much money can be captured by capitalizing on these strategies; that all depends on how much money you are talking vs how much can be gained.

Large company example;
Annual revenues $\underline{\$365,000,000.00}$ = $1,000,000.00
Days in year 365 divided by   1 days sales
   If this one day of sales, $1,000,000.00 could be invested for a year with a return of 6% you would earn $60,000.00. Every little bit helps.

2. **Lock-box system**

It's been around since 1946 but may soon become obsolete do to advances in technology and possible innovations like bitcoin. It reduces mail and processing float. Transit float can be reduced depending on how close the nearest Federal Reserve Bank or their branch is. You ask your customer to mail their check to a numbered post office box provided by a bank. The bank is authorized to open the lock box (which they do every 2 hours every day of the year, depending on volume sometimes every ½ hour), process the checks, and deposit the checks into your account. The check is analyzed, totaled, and scanned. Funds are available for use within one business day. One of your competitors may wait for their funds to come in the mail while you are already using the cash to enhance your business from the same customer.

Compare how that affects the $1,000,000.00 a day in sales vs cash available.

Suppose you could cut the time the normal 5 day through the mail process to the 1 day lock box system. You now have $1,000,000.00 available to you for 4 more days. Let's suppose you invested it in an account that yields the 6% annual percentage rate. The daily interest rate for a 6% annual percentage rate is .000164384. You could multiply it by the daily percentage rate or; $4,000,000.00 X 6% = $240,000.00 divided by 365 gives you $658.00 more money per day. $658 times 4 more days is $2,632.00. By reducing the 5 day wait to one day you increase your cash by $2,632.00. Get the picture? That is now $2,632.00 you would not have had if you didn't have the lock box system.

There are charges for the lock box system, which you should check out to make sure depending on your revenues if it is of value to you.

Cost vs benefit analysis
Benefits of the lock box system;
- Increase working cash; time between having a check paid and sent to you and getting it in your bank
- Eliminating support staff for banking needs, i.e. receiving, endorsing, totaling, and depositing checks
- Chance of documents getting lost is reduced because the paperwork goes through fewer hands
- Bad check warnings are earlier making it possible for you to jump on getting the shipment stopped, canceling it, or stopping it from being delivered until the check is good.
- If the check is cut after delivery you get a chance to get to the customer before they sell any of it and request it to be shipped back or go pick it up before they can sell it to their customers.

GETTING THE MONEY OVER THE FENCE

MAKE SURE THE BENEFITS EXCEED THE COSTS!
Costs of cash management services
Lock box system;

Check processing costs of the new system must be offset by;
Days saved in the collection process (float reduction)
times
Average check amount
times
rate of return earned with the money invested for amount of days saved by using the lock box system.

Here's the mathematical formula
Check processing cost increase for lock box system $.18ea.
Average Check size $1,000.00
Marketable securities return will be   .06%
.06% divided by 365 days =   .000164384
$1,000.00 times .000164384 =   .1644
$.18 divided by .1644   =   1.095 days to break even

If you can speed up your collections by more than 1.095 days it is worth investing in the lock box process.
(PAC's) Pre – Authorized Checks

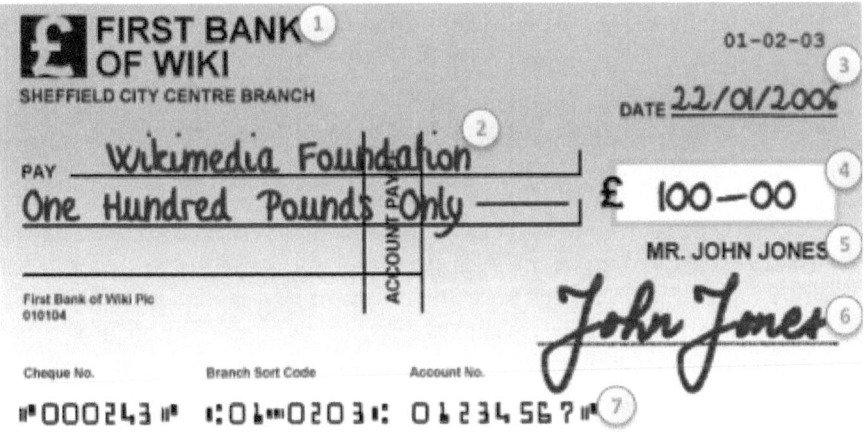

What is a pre – authorized check?
It is just like a regular check except it doesn't require the signature of the person whose account it is drawn on. It is created through legal authorization.

When do you use this?
When you get a lot of checks for the same amount from the same customer.

Who would use this?
How about insurance companies, consumer credit companies, charitable or religious organizations, savings and loans, leasing companies.

How does it work?

a. You are authorized as their customer to draw checks on the companies demand deposit account.

b. You sign an indemnification agreement and send it to the banks that have the demand deposit accounts. The agreement lets the bank know they are to honor the PAC's.

c. A magnetic tape is created containing all necessary information by the company.

d. When the checks are written (weekly, biweekly, monthly) the company keeps a hard copy listing of all tape data.

e. The bank will write the PAC's when they get the tape data. The PAC's will be processed through the commercial banking system. The commercial bank will then return a report to the company letting them know what checks were processed.

Benefits;
- Cash flow can be predicted
- Clerical processing reduced and Postage and billing costs are eliminated
- It's automatic, customers often don't even think about the payment.
- It replaces billing statements
- The company can almost cut out floats
-

Concentration Banking

A bank a company keeps an account in for a large portion of its disbursements. Many companies have multiple locations to deposit checks written to them so they can keep the float time to a minimum. The money is moved to a main account where checks are written. The main account is located in a concentration bank for surplus funds from the multiple locations. The money can be setup to automatically transfer once a certain balance is in the multiple bank locations.

Depository Transfer Checks

These are used with the concentration banking system. These are the checks used to transfer the money from the multiple accounts to the concentration bank.

Benefits;
- Surplus cash does not sit around unused in multiple locations
- How much cash is available is clearer to the higher-level executives so they can use it to keep the company moving forward.
- Funds are easier to track and control
- Money can be transferred quickly to marketable security accounts to earn interest to increase the company's' cash flow

Wire Transfers

Wire transfers are quicker than depository transfer checks. They are the fastest way to transfer money from multiple accounts to the concentration bank.

How are wire transfers done?

Bank wire

A private wire service used by about 250 banks in the USA is used for wire transfers.

Federal Reserve Wire System

Commercial banks who are Members of the Federal Reserve System can use the Fed Wire. A non-member can use the system through its correspondent bank.

Wire transfers differ from depository transfers in that they are requested by the executives of the company rather than automatically issued when excess funds become available.

Wire transfers are much more expensive than depository transfers but happen faster. You should calculate the money that can be made as a result of the quick transfer vs the costs of the wire transfer.

13 CASH OUTFLOW STRATEGIES

How you spend your money is as important as how you collect it. Here are tips on ways to improve your cash flow by spending it wisely.

CASH OUTFLOW MANAGEMENT

ZBA's (Zero balance accounts)
Accounts in local markets that allow the authorized area executive to write checks in a close geographic location.

Who uses them and why?

These accounts are for large companies that have multiple places paying out money.

ZBA's give the company centralized control over the outflows.

- Authorized people write checks from each of their separate accounts. The accounts are empty. They contain no money. Hence the term Zero Balance Accounts.
- These accounts are in the concentration bank.
- All accounts have separate titles, numbers, and statements.
-

Benefits

- Corporate headquarters has full knowledge of all checks that written.
- The local responsible executive has authority to make payments without contacting corporate for approval.
- Surplus funds are non-existent in local accounts.
- It's unnecessary to transfer money to the local account, saving transfer costs.
- Checks clear when paid to a local account, keeping a tight control on where the money goes.
- While the checks clear to the local vendor they may take time to clear the concentration account depending on how far away it is. This leaves the money in the concentration account longer.
-

Payable through drafts

These drafts resemble checks in appearance, are not drawn on bank accounts even though they clear through the banking system, but are legal. Bank serves as an intermediary issuing firm and a demand deposit account. Corporate issuers return all drafts they don't want to pay the day after drafts are issued. Drafts not returned are automatically paid. Signatures, amounts, and dates are checked for validation. Drafts that may be considered inappropriate can be stopped.

Why use them?

To provide for control over payments in the field; the drafts are reviewed before final payment. For example a local agent of an insurance company doesn't have check signing authority. The agent can however issue a draft for a quick settlement, which could be declined if corporate disapproves of the payment.

Transfer of available funds is required by the Federal Reserve System when the drafts are presented. Until the issuing firm approves of the payment, the pass through bank will hesitate to cover the float in case they are not approved. It's a good way to measure available funds.

Remote disbursing

Remote disbursing is a cash management system used to extend the float on disbursements.

How does it work?

It involves a concentration bank and a smaller local bank. The Federal Reserve System has a tough time clearing local checks. Your company would write checks out of the local banks account rather than your concentration bank.

Why? It takes longer to clear and you get a little more float on your money. What's the big deal? It depends on how much money you are talking about. Suppose you have $10,000,000.00 in checks your wrote. It takes an extra day to clear. Your money is earning .06% annually or .0001644% per day. That's $1,644.00 in extra money. Or figured another way its; $10,000,000.00 X .06% = $600,000.00. Divide that by 365 days = $1,644. (Both figures are rounded up to the nearest dollar) Although legal, the Federal Reserve discourages the use of this technique. You also have to be careful about your relationship with your vendor. If it causes a delay in payment in their account, they may want you to choose a different way of paying them.

The preceding covers most <u>techniques</u> in cash management to increase your bottom line. Let's take a look at some techniques using management <u>strategies</u> when purchasing equipment.

14 CASH LEVERAGE STRATEGIES

Equipment

1. **Lease**

What is a lease?

A contract that gives you the use of the equipment without having to pay for it in full when you buy it. You get to use it for a specific period and turn it back to the lesser at the end of the lease. If it is a full service lease you don't have to maintain it, pay for any repairs, taxes, and insurance is carried by the leasing company. If it is a net lease, you absorb these expenses. It can be cancelable or non-cancelable. If the lease is cancelable often there is a penalty.

You may lease your space. This is an operating lease. An operating lease is for a short time and can end with notice from either party.

A financial lease is not cancelable and is for a longer time. You must make payments until the lease ends and turn the equipment back in. Many options are available and you need to consider which one fits your financial picture most.

2. **Sale/leaseback**

[Image: Stylized "Lease Agreement" header with partial visible text: "A lease agreement is a... lessee to pay the lessor for... term rental agreement is... identifies the leased ass... terms under which... ments ar..."]

How does it work?

- You sell an asset to another entity and lease it back from them. It is sold at market value; you get the money and the use of the equipment. Payments are made to the entity, which includes an interest payment to them for the use of their money. Title to the equipment is held by the entity you lease the equipment back from. The entity you lease it from lists it as an asset and at the end of the lease period they can do whatever they want with the equipment. You don't own it so you don't get the benefit of any value it might have at the end of the lease period.

Who does these deals?
- Insurance companies
- Institutional investors
- Finance companies
- Independent leasing companies
-

3. **Direct leasing**

How does it work?

You get to use an asset you didn't buy and don't own. Examples would be; leasing your copier or computer equipment. You don't have to pay all the money for the total cost of the equipment up front. It is similar to getting a loan and paying it off, it can be for the length of the useful life of the equipment or a lease payment period. You are obligated to make the payments.

Who does these deals?
- Manufacturers
- Finance companies
- Banks
- Independent leasing companies
- Special-purpose leasing companies
- Partnerships

All the above except for the manufacturers buy the equipment and lease it to you.

4. **Leverage leasing**

What is it?

A lease for high dollar items. I.e. a train, plane, ship, and things like oil rigs etc… It involves 3 entities. The person (or company) who leases it, the person (or company) who provides money for the lease and the person (or company) that lends the money.

How does it work?

The big difference in a lease like this is the lesser is an equity participant and finances a certain percentage. For example; 80% with a long term lender and provides a 20% equity investment for the purchase of the equipment and then leases it to you. The lesser is also a borrower.

15 TERM LOANS

Term loans

What are they?

Most term financing comes from commercial banks. The difference between a term loan from a bank and other types of business loans are;

1. A term loan matures over one year.
2. Credit is extended in most cases through a formal loan agreement.
3. Payment is made most often through periodic payments; quarterly, semiannually, or annually. The payment schedule matched to the person or company's cash flow. Payments can be made in equal installments or irregular amounts or in one lump sum. Payment can be made like a mortgage with a balloon payment at the end. Most have 3 to 5 year maturities.

How do they work?

You pay more in interest for a term loan than a short-term loan. The reason is there is more risk for the lender is because their money is out for a longer time. You will find; covenants in your agreement. These are stipulations you have to abide by to keep your loan in force.

Restrictions;
- Prohibit you from getting behind on other loans
- Demand for full payment, which might put you out of business and them out of getting their money back.
- Might want to adjust the interest rate or terms.
- May want you to maintain a minimum amount of working capital.
- Want to limit cash dividends or common stock restrictions.
- May want limited capital expenditures by fixing a dollar amount or an amount equal to depreciation charges.
- Could limit your long term debt.
- You may need to provide financial statements regularly.
- You may be restricted in how you leverage your accounts receivable and lease agreements.
- Use of the money may be stipulated in the agreement
- You may be asked to carry life insurance on an executive
- Bonuses and compensation may be limited during the life of the loan.

Keep in mind, the more you know about money and how it works, how the banks money works the fewer restrictions you are likely to have because you understand the ins and outs of the financing choices.

The interest rate can either be;

- Fixed for the life of the loan
- Variable, which fluctuates with the rates in the economy. Often you can get the bank to put a ceiling on how high the interest rate they charge can go. They will put the lowest rate they will charge.

Expect to pay the bank's legal expenses incurred for drawing up the paperwork for the loan. Fees can range between a quarter and three quarter of a percent.

Benefits;
- You deal with the lender
- The loan can be customized to your needs
- Your bank will judge you on your past borrowing successes.
- The terms and conditions can be revised if your situation changes

- It is easier than floating a public issue and most times smaller firms can't approach the capital market because of their minimal size.

Revolving Credit Agreements

What are they?

It is a commitment by a bank to lend up to a certain amount of money for a specific period.

How do they work?

90-day agreements that can be renewed. The length of the agreement could be as long as 3 years. Interest rates are higher than a short-term loan. The bank commits to always have the money available for the length of the agreement. The banks often charge a commitment fee for this accommodation. You can set it up so it converts to a term loan during the life of the loan or when the revolving credit agreement ends convert it to a term loan.

When would you use this?

You would use this when you are not clear about how much money you will need over an unclear period. For example: you may introduce a new product over the next few years and you don't know how much will sell. You would consider a revolving credit loan.

Insurance company term loans

What are they?

Terms loans that do not mature before 7 years and if you try to pay them early, you could get penalized. Why 7 years or more? They don't have other income from loans coming in from the borrower so they want to get paid back their full interest payments. Interest rates are higher because of the length of the loan and more costs are involved at higher risk.

16 ASSET LEVERAGE STRATEGIES

Sale of excess assets

Take a look at your assets. Do you have any assets you could sell and continue to operate your business? If you have assets that no longer serve a productive purpose for the effective operation of your business, consider liquidating the asset.

Transfer of lender to pay debt

You may find you can change to a different lender to get more favorable terms. Consider splitting debt among over one lender to decrease each debtor's risk and get the interest rate you are paying lower.

Real Estate

Sale/leaseback

You or your firm may own real estate that you could sell to an investor who may lease it back to you. At the end of the lease period the lesser realizes any residual value, which would have been yours before the sale to the investor. There is a tax advantage; land is not depreciable but lease payments are tax deductible. You can expense or depreciate the cost of the land.

Who does these?
- Insurance companies
- Institutional investors
- Finance companies
- Independent leasing companies

Mortgage bonds

What are they?

It is a bond (which is a debt instrument) secured by a lien on property.

How does it work?

The mortgage bond is issued for less than the value of the real estate. In case the value of the property decreases the bondholders are protected to some degree if the property is worth more than the bond when they lend the money. If there is a foreclosure on the property the bondholders can sell the property to get their money back. If the sale of the property does not cover the loans (bonds) from the investors the bondholders become general creditors.

17 SELL STOCK TO GET MONEY

Going Public

STOCK

Selling ownership in your company to investors

You've heard stories of companies who have gone public return to private companies. Going public it isn't always the solution you may look for, but many times it is the right solution.

Even if you are a small company you should be aware of what is involved in selling stock in case you have contacts that want to own equity in your company. When you proceed through this experience your accounting firm, legal firm and board of directors will be advising you about the details.

Here's a general overview on how you take a company public!

You need to be a corporation. In your articles of incorporation or Certificate of Incorporation it needs to list the following details;

- Name of the corporation
- Purpose and nature of its business
- Authorized numbers of shares of capital stock may be issued with descriptions of various classes of stock
- Amount of indebtedness the corporation may incur
- Statement of the duties and officers of the corporation
- Names and addresses of the original directors

To get listed on the New York Stock Exchange you must qualify as follows;

- At least, 1,100,000 shares publicly held shares with market value of at least $18,000,000
- A minimum of 2,000 round lot shareholders (100 shares or more) or 2,200 shareholders
- An average monthly trading volume of at least 100,000 shares for the most recent six months
- Minimum pre-tax earnings of $2,500,000 for the latest fiscal year

Besides the above qualifiers there should be;

- A national interest in your company
- Your company must solicit proxies
-

You can also list your company on the OTC (over the counter) market or the NASDAQ (national association of securities dealers automated quotation system).

The stockholders elect the board of directors. The board appoints a management team to help them govern the corporation.

You can raise capital either by issuing stock or bond securities. Stock is an actual investment in your company; an investor owns a portion of your company. The portion they own of your company is relative to how much stock they own. A bond is a loan from an investor or group of investors. Bondholders don't own a portion of your company.

When you first offer sale of your company's stock it is an *i*nitial *p*ublic *o*ffering (IPO).

Should you and your board decide you want to own some of the stock being offered it is called treasury stock.

The SEC (Securities and Exchange Commission) makes sure your company is registered. They don't declare your company a sound or unsound investment they regulate the issue of stock. You are required to give them and anyone who wants to buy stock in your company a prospectus. It covers all the details about your company. The day the SEC receives your documents is known as the filing date. After the filing date there is a cooling off period of 20 days. This is to make sure there is no misleading information and the filings are complete. During this cooling off period a red herring (preliminary prospectus) is prepared by the issuer. It has a red border on the cover letting the potential investor know a registration statement has been filed with the SEC but is not in effect yet.

This new issue is sold through a syndicate of investment bankers called an underwriting syndicate. These investment bankers bring the buyers and sellers together. The investment bankers get as much money for the stock as they can. They buy your stock and sell it to the public. If they buy all of your stock, it is called a firm commitment underwriting. They assume all the risk and are betting the public will pay more for it than they paid for the stock. If they don't sell all the stock, they bought they have to absorb the difference. If they agree to sell as much as possible they can return the balance of unsold stock to you, this is called a best efforts underwriting. Suppose you decide you need all the money from the sale of the stock being offered. You tell the syndicate you want a best efforts all-or-none deal, which means they return it all to you if they can't sell all of it, the shares that were sold are cancelled. As soon as the SEC has declared the issue registered, the investment bankers go to work selling the stock they bought of yours to the public. They get their money through the difference between how much they paid for the stock and how much they can sell it for. Suppose they bought it from you for $22 and sold it for $25, the $3.00 difference is the spread, which is what they get paid and why they do it.

JAMES S WITTMACK

18 Sell bonds to get money

BONDS

> **VICTORIA.**
>
> **The Church of Christ, Boronia.**
>
> Issue of 100 Debentures of £5 without Interest.
>
> *No.* 1 **DEBENTURE.** £5.
>
> The Board of Officers of the Church of Christ at Boronia in the State of Victoria for itself and its successors agrees with the holder of this Debenture as follows:—
> 1. The total number of Debentures issued is 100 each of the value of £5.
> 2. No interest is payable on or in respect of such debentures.
> 3. The Board will in the month of February in each year hereafter ballot for the payment of 10 of the debentures of the value of £5.
> 4. The Board will within thirty days after the taking of such ballot pay to the holder of the debentures selected by such ballot the face value thereof in cash.
> 5. The numbers of the debentures so selected will be published by the "Australian Christian."
> 6. The holders of debentures may register their names and addresses and the numbers of the debentures held by them with the Secretary of the Church and upon the selection of any of the debentures so registered for payment the Secretary will forthwith notify the holder thereof.
>
> DATED at Boronia this *First* day of *April* 1921
>
> For and on behalf of the Board of Officers.
>
> *F. J. Goodwin* Evangelist.
> *J. Maguire* Secretary.

Getting loans for your company from lenders

A bond offering is a promise to pay back an amount you borrow. U.S. Government

Municipal and corporate bonds

All unique in their structure. Corporate bonds are the ones you will issue as a company owner. You are promising to pay a fixed amount of interest each year for a fixed period. At the end of that time you promise to pay the face value of the bond to the bondholder. For example, suppose you are issuing a bond with a $10,000.00 face amount with a maturity date of 10 years. The bondholder gives you $10,000.00. During the 10 years you pay them an agreed upon interest rate for the use of their money. After 10 years are you give them their $10,000.00 back.

You buy the bond back sooner than the agreed upon time. This allows you to avoid paying interest for the full time. The bondholder rarely likes to have the bonds called (redeemed) before the full term because they don't get all their interest as stated in their original agreement when they loaned the money to your company. To protect the bondholder most bonds are not callable for at least 5 to 10 years. If the bonds are called, you often pay a premium to pay them off before they mature. The premium compensates them for the interest they will lose when you redeem them before the maturity date.

Bondholders get first dibs on interest paid over stockholders. The bondholder has first claim to proceeds of a corporation's assets who has filed bankruptcy. Bondholders claims also precede general creditors.

File with the SEC before the public offering of the bonds.

A bank or trust company is appointed as the trustee. They are the representative of the bondholder and acts in their best interest.

CORPORATE BONDS

Corporate bonds are listed on an exchange. However, large quantities of corporate issues are not listed securities so you would find them on the over-the-counter market.

Types of Corporate Bonds

Guaranteed Bonds

Secured by an additional corporation if the borrowing corporation defaults.

Income Bonds (adjustment bonds)

Interest payments are not promised and companies in bankruptcy issue these. The issuer will pay interest only if it has sufficient funds. A bond investor gets a higher return because of the obvious risk involved with these.

Zero-coupon bonds

No periodic interest is paid. All money is paid on maturity.

Junk Bonds (speculative bonds)

These pay a high return because they are the highest risk bonds. Often these are companies direly need money or are for companies that have little potential to pay the bondholder back.

Secured bonds

An asset is pledged to protect the bondholder from default.

Mortgage Bonds

Property is used as an asset to protect the bondholder from default.

Equipment Trust Certificates

Equipment can be the asset to protect bondholders from default.

Collateral Trust Bonds

Securities that can be collateral to protect bondholders from default.

Unsecured Bonds

Debentures

Bondholders trust the good faith of the corporation to pay them back. There is nothing else protecting the bondholders in case of default.

Convertible Debentures

These let the bondholders convert their bonds to stock

Eurobonds

Bonds sold in another country. Not the country whose currency where the bond is issued.

19 Alternative financial sources to get money

You already know about money sources like, friends, family and fools as the capital market refers to your start up sources of funding. Before I get into alternative financial sources like; private investors, angels, investment bankers, PEG's (private equity groups) the 3 types of venture capitalists and institutional investors let me take a moment to give you some background on why all these investors exist, when and where they came.

Why they exist is easy; they want to grow their money by investing in you.

When did this concept get started?

Let's first talk about ABL's. They lend money based on what you have available in collateral. The most familiar Asset Based Lender to you may be your local bank. There are many more options available with much more flexibility.

ABL's have been around for over 50 years. Only in the last 10 years have they become serious contenders to banks. This is serious money, in 1990 ABL's accounted for around $96 billion in lending, today it's around $326 billion. That doesn't include factors around $96 billion today up from $52 billion in 1990.

One of the main reasons ABL's have become an alternative to traditional bank lending is the businesses they lend to are far greater in scope. For instance, a bank won't get involved in high tech and an ABL will.

Why does a business owner consider an ABL instead of a bank? To get more sleep. I'm serious about that! Entrepreneurs often stay up or wake up in the wee hours of the night to noodle over how to get money to help them with existing bills or to help them with their acquisition plans or working capital.

Their bank has turned them down, they are clueless about how to get money from the capital market or they don't qualify yet.

The good and the bad.

THE GOOD

Provide more leverage than bank loans ABL's are more familiar with your business model and gets involved more as a partner. Their close monitoring enables them to establish a closer relationship with you.

- Provide consistency of financing
- Impose fewer covenants
- Higher level of commitment
- Relationship is more personal; ratio is often 15-to-1 as opposed to 100-to-1 in banks

- Rarely secure their loans
- Because they need less, they monitor more which makes it possible for them to lend more

THE BAD

Due-diligence process is unfamiliar to many entrepreneurs and seems burdensome to the novice

Costs are higher due to the frequency of reports and contact, but this allows you to get more money from them so it is often worth it.

More frequent progress check ups, however, these in reality help the entrepreneur stay on top of their game and become sensitive to issues affecting their business they might not pay attention to.
Updates are time consuming

How do you tap in to the investor / lender in the capital market?

Private investors, angels, PEG's (groups of angels, private equity groups) investment bankers, 3 types of venture capitalists and institutional investors?

Over 80% of all startup companies get funding through informal sources of funding, such as associates, friends, and private "Angel" investors.

There are over 6700 VC's in the United States with over $200 Billion under management; 5 times that much from global sources. Over 600 plus PEG's. How come you don't know them? Well, one reason might be YOU ARE TRYING TO SUCCEED IN BUSINESS by running it rather than out networking with investors as a full time career. If you want to avoid having your business plan end up in the receptionist trash can you better have a formal introduction into the capital market. Sure, you can attend breakfast meetings and give your presentation, try to convince various investors to look at your offering. It is a full time job. Let me get you up to speed on how the capital market works.

You have heard of VC's or even had dealings with them. Which type of VC have you dealt with? The public or private VC firm? or the corporate VC division?

The average VC firm receives hundreds if not thousands of business plans a year. They only fund four to six a year. Unless the well-written financing proposal is presented by a firm who specializes in networking relationships with the capital market as a full time job with the investment community. If you are represented by one of those types of firms, your plan gets read because the investor has given the firm a profile of the type of investment they are looking for and your company fits that profile. Who would you rather lend money to? Someone who came to you highly recommended by a firm you trust and have ultimate confidence in? or some guy who thinks their idea is a good fundable opportunity?

Seed stage funding; early or start-up financing for completion of product development: often for companies who are no farther along than the idea stage.

Second Stage financing; for an established business that needs additional working capital to help them grow.

Third-Stage Funding is for expanding facilities or fueling marketing and sales efforts.

Fourth Stage or Bridge Financing is funding for a company that is on the path to taking their company public. Bridge financing covers the costs of hiring investment banks to structure the IPO and promote the offering. This is repaid with the proceeds of the IPO and used to restructure earlier equity positions.

    Acquisition/Buyout Financing: $3,000,000 - $20,000,000.

    Acquisition: Funds provided to finance the acquisition of another company. Also high interest "Junk" Bonds may be used or substantial debt from banks.

Leveraged Buyout (LBO): Funds provided to allow a management group to buy a product line or business from a public or private company. Revitalized management may have as little as 1% of their own money invested.

Research and Planning requirements for every <u>START UP</u>

1. Feasibility studies
    Should your venture even be attempted?
2. Business Plan
    Required for financing
    Required for investment – operation rounds
3. Debt and equity ratios
    What are your optimum ratios?
4. Operational plan
    Plan to get your company up and running

5. Funding Sources
   Debt and equity
6. Project evaluations
   Pre – Post investments analysis
7. Exit Strategies

Mergers, acquisitions, IPO's, LBO's, ESOP's

YOUR DEAL

Each part of your deal affects the other

1. Is early investor return of capital included?
2. There are risks involved, and the amount you pay an investor depends on their perception of risk in your company. How is the premium for risk calculated?
3. Are there other incentives that may not be monetary being offered?
4. What are the options to increase an investor's equity share or liquidate early?
5. How have you handled tax, legal and state securities issues?
6. What is the organizational format of your company?
7. What is your exit strategy?
8. Have you handled all the risks involved with personnel issues? Things like, key man insurance, buy-sell agreements, convertible preferred stock, management contract agreements?
9. How will capital infusion from outside sources affect the stock value?
10. How will the dilution of stock affect ownership percentages?

Each one of these affects the other so they all must be addressed in your deal structure.

20 How to get money from VC's, Investment Bankers, Angel Investors, PEG's (private equity groups)

VENTURE CAPITAL

The structure of a VC firm

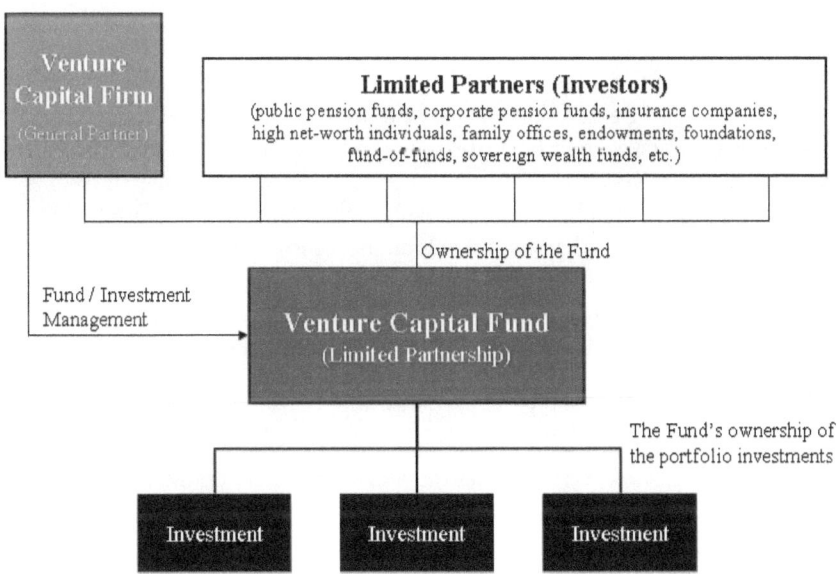

Let's address this misunderstood and misquoted source of funding first.

VC's are known by some as "Vulture Capitalists" to some entrepreneurs because they ended up not owning their company or even working for them. Those deals that are more sensationalized than those that go through without a hitch.

What is Venture Capital?

Money provided by professionals who invest in growing companies that have potential.

Where did it come from?

The money is from; private and public pension funds, endowment funds, foundations, corporations, wealthy individuals, foreign investors, and the venture capitalists.

History of Venture Capital

After WWII the US government realized there was a need for riskier investors than banks. The Small Business Investment Company (SBIC) was created in the mid 50s. Legislation allowed SBICs to leverage their private capital up to 3-1. In 1976 that increased to 4-1 by borrowing from the fed below market interest rates.

About the same time venture capital firms started forming private partnerships outside the SBIC. The private VC's recognized the SBIC is rigid because it has to comply with government regulations. Because the VC sources are more flexible, they are able to help businesses out more. An example would be not having a size limitation for the amount they want to invest. To protect the government, the SBIC does have limitations. Private VC's exceeded SBICs in total capital under management relatively quickly. Within 10 years VC's exceeded SBIC's total capital under management.

In the late 70s and early 80's only large established companies could afford to fund the development of new products. Hence the better known companies became recognized for product advances quicker than the smaller less capitalized companies. Because large companies are so full of politics and processes new innovations were slowing considerably. It's been said, "Give a large company an innovation to launch and they can get it done in 3 years, when the more nimble entrepreneur can get it done in 8 mo's. or less."

Investors recognized this and realized the returns that could be made by investing in lesser known companies could be significant. They just needed the capital to get it going.

Venture Capitalists want to exit quickly, take a company public to do so or merge or be acquired often before the companies are ready. That's why you hear about VC's wanting their people in charge. If management isn't structured correctly the VC's exit strategy won't work. If it doesn't work they have the potential to lose money.

What do VC's look for?

Start - Ups
- High growth companies
- Expertise of the management team
- Ability to execute the business plan
- Market leading products/services
- Potential to gain significant market share
- Underutilized fast growing market segment

Proven Companies
- Strong Management
- Stability of revenues
- Adequate cash flow
- Expectation for operational improvements
- Expectation for cost reductions
- Potential to increase size
- Potential to increase profitability
- Potential for merger or acquisition

Types of companies

Computer Technology
Medical/health
Telecommunications

That doesn't mean other industries aren't looked at, it simply means other industries need to meet the VC's criteria and be looking for $7,000,000 to $20,000,000 or more. Why? The costs of due diligence and valuing a company exceed the return if a company is looking for less money.

There are ways to get VC money if a company is looking for less, one way is to have a credentialed valuation completed for revue by the VC. A credentialed valuator is licensed to tell the truth. If the VC is looking at the truth this limits the money they need to spend on due diligence.

What is the typical process?

Expect to have many intensive meetings. Be prepared to provide lots of documentation. The VC is backing you and your team, if you or your team don't pass the test you or a member may not get to be part of the funded deal.

Should you evaluate the VC?

Yes. Make sure they understand your market and business plan. Here's a possible scenario to be prepared for: Suppose it is 18 months after your first meeting. You have a check on the table for $4,000,000. The VC and their attorneys want to change some items you discussed and agreed to at this final meeting.

If you get the money, should you take it?

They change highlight the items you discussed. They present the corrected document for your review and suggest you just read the changed highlighted items. On a whim you decide just for the heck of it to check the rest of the document. You find they also changed things they said they weren't going to change. The changes materially affect ownership and control. Should you take the money? It's 18 months later, you have no other sources, and you are on the edge of going broke.

Unfortunately it is at this point you may regret not engaging a professional to handle this transaction, but it's way too late if you are out of money. Often they charge for work they do but you get caught up in their costs rather than their benefits.

From Last to First

Usually you will find start up money from "Angels" who are private individuals who fund companies in the early stages. They aren't as cut throat as VC's, however, they have their own set of frustrating issues. The biggest frustration is; each one has their own way of doing things. So if you get more than one angel involved you will often have to deal with each angel's issues separate and differently from the other. If you are properly prepared you can manage their differences.

How to succeed with Angels

Be properly prepared

1. Have a brief presentation
2. Presentation should address, product/service, market, management team, reason for your product/service
3. Present to trusted individuals to get feedback
4. Tape it to see if you present your case clearly
5. Make sure your case is compelling
6.

Know who you are talking to

1. Get references
2. If you stay local, check with people you know
3. If you want to go out of your local area, establish a relationship with a trusted firm that has outside area contacts
4. You'll have to go to network meetings and present many times before actual funding
5. Angels are often slow to move and many times move in small amounts not significant enough to get the jump start you need
6. There are exceptions but expect a lot of nitpicking
7.

What will you need?

1. Term sheet – a one page outline of the investment opportunity
2. L.O.I. (Letter of Intent) is another summary. Often investors prefer the term sheet because it is not as legally binding as the L.O.I.
3. Valuation - If you haven't had a professional firm complete a valuation include your best estimate of your company's value.
4. Full Disclosure – make sure you comply with disclosing risks involved according to your state securities regulations
5. Common or preferred stock?
    a. Common – puts investor on equal footing with the you
    b. Preferred – Savvy investors choice – this puts them as a high priority for repayment

Investment Bankers

Fees range from 3% to 6% typically of the total price or investment. Performance incentives are often added. For complex deals retainers are often applied. Investment bankers usually invest in companies that have been around a while and have strong EBITDA (Earning before interest, taxes, depreciation and amortization.) Investment bankers are looking for deals that are sound opportunities with a proven track record. Rarely does an investment banker show an interest in a startup. They may know angels that might be interested and steer them in your direction.

Equity vs Debt

Equity is money from the stock market
Value of assets minus liabilities
An investor is buying a piece of your company
What do investors want? Dividends and their stock value to increase
No guarantee
Debt is money from the bond market
IOU a specific interest rate for your money
Investor expects scheduled payments for their money
If it's a bond, when it matures the investor gets their money back in addition to the interest payments
Investor risks; Interest rates could go up but they are stuck with your agreement

Pros and Cons of equity vs debt

Stocks are riskier but they offer potentially better investment performance. Equity returns are volatile. Inflation and interest rate risks are greater with bonds.

Your hunt for money is a challenging one, and often a reason entrepreneurs choose professionals to help them.

Private Investors, Angel's, Private Equity Groups (PEG's) work in a similar way. Investment Bankers, Private – Public and Institutional VC's work in a similar way. Institutional Investors are often VC divisions of larger corporations.

Regardless of which direction you choose, if it is your first time it would be in your best interest to engage a professional who is familiar with the language of the investment community who can guide you through the maze minimizing collateral damage.

21 The do's and don'ts of pitching your company

Talk to over one lender even if the first one you talk to will lend you the money. Google founders met with 81 investors before they found the right investors. Compare the terms of their offer and make sure they are the best terms you can get. You will find if the first lender you talk to wants to give you money then more lenders will.

You may find you have to talk to many lenders before you get the first offer. Sometimes this is just because there are problems with the data in your plan, or you haven't rehearsed it often enough for you to do it and can deflect concerns and answer questions without hesitation. Each time you talk to another lender you will get more confidence and get better at presenting your plan. Keep this in mind when shopping your plan around. Choose a lender or two you may not want money from just to rehearse your presentation for the lender you would like to get the money from.

DON'T FORGET THIS!

During the meetings with lenders you are just trying to find out if they will loan you the money. They are trying to decide if they can loan it to you. You must remember to focus on helping them get what they want. If they think you will give them what they want, then they will be more amenable to giving you what you want.

What do they want? Money

What do you want? Return on their loan or investment; Money

You need each other. You both want the same things but want to get it in different ways.

The money they want is interest or increase in equity on the money they loan to you. The money you want is the money they loan to you.

Your job is to convince them if they loan you the money they will get the money they want for loaning it to you. You will do this by showing them a professional business plan. Having all the answers to their questions. That's why you have to be involved in the planning and data gathering of your planning process, either by reviewing each piece of data connected to these two issues or doing them yourself.

The do's and don'ts of pitching your company

GETTING THE MONEY OVER THE FENCE

1. HARD NUMBERS - unless you have the data and hard numbers to back up your projections and needs, investors won't be able to commit

Don't Say: "I'm going to need more money because a lot of people have said they want to do more business with me."

Say: "I need $100,000 to buy faster equipment to accept orders from my two largest clients who are planning to increase their orders by 25 percent over the next 12 months."

2. EXCELLENT RESEARCH
Explain how, who and why. How you arrived at your numbers. Who research sources are. Why you believe it to be the best measure or indicator. The more data and supporting evidence the better.

Don't Say: "More and more customers are asking for sandwiches."

Say: "As you can see on these charts according to our analysis of 12 months of customer-spending data shows that people are buying 30 percent more sandwiches than a year ago."

3. REASONS YOU ARE THE EXPERT
Make sure you show your credentials by how long you've been in the business and how much research you've done to support your business. Would you put your money behind someone who doesn't understand the fundamentals of the industry they are in? Neither will investors or lenders.

Don't Say: "I always had dolls when I was growing up, so I started my doll business."

Say: "After 10 years of experience in a retail toy stores, and making dolls all my life, I saw a gap in the doll market I knew I could fill."

4. PASSION THAT SHOWS
Let investors and lenders know your business is meaningful to you. Would you want to invest/lend to an entrepreneur who isn't committed to the success of the business and passionate about what they do? Would you invest/lend to an entrepreneur who is only after money?

Why
- do you love your business?
- it is important?
- do you believe in it?

Don't Say: "A friend needed a business development partner, and I didn't have anything else to do."

Say: "I believe that children should have a healthy meal every day and this is the fundamental driver of my business."

5. A MEMORABLE CLOSING

When giving an elevator pitch, entrepreneurs are often so focused on delivering the right information with the right data that when it comes to the end they wind up saying, "So, that's my business… any questions?" The closing is the opportunity for you to say where you want to go next, and draw the investor into a longer conversation or follow-up. Keep it strong and on point.

Don't Say: "Okay, So, what do you think?"

Say: "Nothing would make me more proud than to build a successful company with funding from a firm like yours who believes in my product/service who I can depend on to grow their profits as I grow mine. The financial backing will be the foundation to a great future. What are our next steps? Is meeting Tuesday or Wednesday next week better?"

22 BANK CEO TELLS YOU HOW TO GET MONEY FROM BANKS

Dan C. Yates
CEO
Endeavor Bank
760-795-1250
5/27/03 updated 10/18/18

What to expect if you apply for a Business Loan at Endeavor Bank

Mr. Yates stressed that the approval of a loan request at his Bank is heavily weighted on a company's historical financial performance (Endeavor Bank looks for a company to have a consistent record of profitable operations) and they prefer to lend to companies that have a strong Balance Sheet (specifically they look to see how well capitalized a company is, and the quantity and quality of business assets, relative to the loan request). In addition, the personal net worth of the business owner is always taken into consideration and some loans are approved primarily on the basis of the size and composition of the owner's personal net worth.

Endeavor Statement of Strength

Endeavor offers; ideas, suggestions, strategic planning and SWOT type analysis (i.e. a report that outlines the strengths, weaknesses, opportunities, and threats of a given company. This is developed in conjunction with the client's input for those business owners that request this type of an assessment on their company).

Endeavor Bank is designed for entrepreneurs who want a relationship with a Banker that clearly understands the challenges, goals, and needs of an entrepreneur. The Bankers at Endeavor do indeed because they invested their own money to start Endeavor Bank so they relate to fellow entrepreneurs (because these bankers are themselves, entrepreneurs). As risk takers themselves, these bankers understand fellow business owners on a much deeper level compared to "career bankers" who have never taken the risk to start their own Business.

Endeavor Bank believes in offering general business advice to help entrepreneurs improve their bottom lines. This advice is drawn upon years of experience (that has evolved into knowledge) from serving thousands of closely held businesses (and their owners) from a wide array of different industries.

As a Business Bank, started by banker-entrepreneurs, Endeavor feels they set themselves apart from other banks primarily by the quality of their bankers and the advice these professionals can offer, and the vast network of contacts (these bankers have) which business owners can tap into and leverage as needed.

Endeavor does not charge a fee for their "general business advisory services" as they feel it is the quality and value of this type of advice that that serves as the glue in building and maintaining long-term mutually beneficial business relationships.

Most Banks that Endeavor competes with are hard pressed to offer this same type of advice and guidance due to the lack of skilled bankers in the industry that have the requisite skills and business experience to operate effectively in this arena.

Bankers that do have such skills and experience are few and far between and (if you should happen to meet one) you will typically find that they are assigned to usually serve only the very largest, most sophisticated businesses, with revenues in excess of $100 Million.

Hence at Endeavor, small to mid-sized businesses and their owners, have access to highly trained and skilled bankers that prefer to work with smaller businesses, while their counterparts in the industry spend their time with much larger companies.

It is also worth noting that another advantage in working with Endeavor Bank is that business owners have an opportunity to develop a personal relationship with the CEO of the Bank and thus the business owner will have direct access to the final decision making the authority of the Bank.

Q.   What amount would be the minimum business loan you would consider?

A.   The Bank has no minimum size loan that it will consider (in fact many of the Bank's clients do not have any need to borrow money but are nonetheless important clients for the bank as they maintain good depository accounts), but realistically $25,000 is about the smallest commercial loan request I have seen since we opened the bank, with the exception of a "business overdraft protection line of credit" or a "credit card" which could be as little as $1,000.

Endeavor Bank prefers to work with companies that have a minimum of 2 – 3 million in revenues (sales) and usually a maximum of around $50 Million to $75MM in revenues (sales).

When the Bank receives a loan request that exceeds 10 million dollars, it becomes a challenge for Endeavor Bank to handle a request of this size due to our legal lending limits (currently $6,000,000). We can usually partner up with another bank and share a 50/50 pro-rata interest in large loan participations but at some point, we can not attract a participant if we have only a small percentage of the loan.

Endeavor Bank rarely attempts to fund loans where the total loan commitment is over $10,000,000, and in fact EB prefers to make loans within its legal lending limit of $6,000,000 or less.

Q.   What kind of business owner scenario is most compatible with your banking goals?

A.   A business owner that has operated his company successfully for at least 5 years and is seeking a relationship with a banker that can offer helpful ideas and suggestions.

Q.   Could you put a dollar amount to the size of the loans you offer?

A. Loan amounts from $100,000 to $6,000,000 are in the "zone".
Average size loan is $1,000,000
Average usage on a revolving line of credit is $500,000

Q. *Are loans at Endeavor Bank approved by the loan officer or a consortium?*

A. We only employ very experienced loan officers which are indicative of their years of experience and knowledge. All of our bankers are qualified to determine whether or not a loan request meets the Bank's underwriting criteria and can usually give a quick reply to the business owner that stops just short of a formal loan commitment.

To actually formally approve a loan, we use a quorum system that usually requires the President, or CEO and Chief Credit Officer to approve a loan; Sometimes we might involve all 3 in a loan approval if there is a policy exception.

Q. *Does an entrepreneur need a business plan to get a loan?*

A. We prefer to see one, however, a majority of the more successful seasoned companies that have been in business for an extended period of time we deal with don't utilize business plans. In these situations they have years of financials and history in business (i.e. the norm), the bank interviews the business owner to determine the major components of what would normally be found in a business plan.

> Through our advisory style of relationship banking, we usually uncover
> pretty much all of the pertinent data we need to understand the strengths,
> weaknesses, opportunities, and threats of the businesses we are considering
> lending money to.
>
> This knowledge of the business is then backed up by our review and analysis of the company's financial statements.
>
> Because the businesses we prefer to fund have a minimum of 5 years worth
> of operating performance, the financial statements are critical to our analysis.

As a general rule, when we do receive business plans from established companies, Murphy's Law seems to hold that the thicker the plan is, the
less likely the loan will ultimately be approved and the more likely "words" are being substituted in lieu of historical positive operating performance that would enable the company's qualifications for a loan
approval, to speak for itself;

Also, long business plans often serve to highlight that the owner is struggling to clarify the key points about his business and is instead of rambling or being repetitive.

Q. *On an existing business what kinds of qualifications are you looking for?*

A. To begin with, we look for a business track record of consistent profitability. A minor operating loss within the past three years is ok, provided that owner can 1) offer a good explanation (i.e. lesson learned, but remember the price of tuition in business is often very high and can result in bankruptcy) and 2) If there is a loss in the recent past, we want to see a demonstrated turnaround with profits restored and the business back on track.

We also want to see a strong primary source of repayment for each loan request and a good secondary source of repayment, should the primary source fail to materialize. As an example, the Primary repayment source might be the projected or historical cash flow from the business and the secondary source of repayment might be the collateral that is pledged.

We want to understand the business. It should be made clear during our loan interview, why the business is economically viable. We want to know why the company exists in the face of competition. Does the business have a unique product or niche, perhaps superior service, price advantage, etc.?

Does the business have the "right stuff" to be successful? Does it appear likely that it is going to be around for another five years or longer?

We prefer to lend to companies where we have a good grasp of what the company does, how its product(s) work, what makes its services special. If we cannot understand the business, we probably should not lend money to it.

Management strength and integrity is very important in our loan interview and decision-making process. If we note that management has certain weaknesses, we look to see if they have attempted to compensate for their weaknesses by surrounding themselves with staff that has the strengths or skills they lack.

Q. *What is the number one concern you have when you are considering loaning money to a business?*

A. Getting paid back

Q. *What is the number one problem entrepreneurs with a business plan face when applying for a business loan?*

A. They don't know how to communicate what and how their business does what it does, effectively, to a banker. They also don't know how to think about the act of lending money from the banker's perspective. They should focus more effort in the plan, on helping the banker see where the risk of non-performance on the loan repayment might be, and how said risks of loan default have been mitigated by the business owner, the collateral being offered, or the owner's personal liquidity or significant personal net worth. This is where a plan is very helpful, as a plan helps the Banker know all the things the banker is looking for in approving a loan and hence it prepares the banker for the loan interview when he meets with us.

Q. *Regarding the individuals who are looking for money for their business. What kind of obstacles surface?*

A. They need to have a thorough knowledge of their business that they can effectively and succinctly communicate to a banker.... better yet, bankers would prefer to see a well-written business plan that acknowledges where the holes in the business model are and how management / the business owner, intends to fill them.

The biggest obstacle is when a business owner confuses what they perceive to be a bankable credit risk for what is, in reality, an equity risk. If the risk of non-performance is high (due to an inability to repay the loan because the primary repayment source failed to materialize), then what the business owner really needs is an equity partner, not a lender. A good banker will steer the client in the right direction. If equity is needed, there may be numerous places to obtain it.

Q. *What are you looking for in an entrepreneur who comes to you for money for their business?*

A. We are very impressed by an entrepreneur who makes it clear that repaying the bank loan is of the highest priority and the borrower will find numerous ways to assure the banker that the risk of non-payment is nearly zero. This can be accomplished by offering personal guarantees, collateral, etc.,.

Occasionally, a banker will meet someone who has a bankruptcy in their past. This is normally the kiss of death in trying to reestablish credit and getting a loan approved.

One way to turn a negative experience (bankruptcy) into a positive is to demonstrate to the bank that you went back (after the bankruptcy was discharged) and reinstated the debts that were "forgiven" (the timing of this reinstatement would normally coincide with the time where you are once again back on your feet and doing very good financially).

If a person with a bankruptcy sets out to make restitution (because you feel strongly that all debts should be repaid even if the courts legally wipe the record clean) and accomplishes same, most bankers will overlook the B.K.

We also like to know about an entrepreneur's biggest challenge, to date in their business career, and how did they overcome it?

Q. *What are some key problems an entrepreneur should have solutions for in their plan?*

A. How to overcome fierce competition.
Unforeseen increases in costs or dilution in gross margins
Large customer concentrations
Have a plan if the company's product niche ends
Have a plan to reinvent the company, if necessary
Business owners should openly share concerns and potential solutions

I like to read all the things that can go wrong in a business plan and want to see what the business owner indicates he can and might be able to do about these concerns if things do go wrong.

Q. *What about the financials, what is the weight of importance in a plan?*

A. Greatest Weight

Q. *What financial reports do you like to see in a plan?*

A. Historical Financial Statements prepared on an accrual basis going back 3 to 5 years

A Source/Use of cash funds flow statement

A monthly cash flow forecast with the cumulative borrowing need set forth at the bottom, showing how the bank loans will be drawn down (i.e. the purpose of the loan) and the estimated time period as to when the loan is repaid (i.e. reflects the anticipated primary source of repayment).

Bottom line is we want to see a Realistic financial picture not a pie in the sky projections. Be conservative. This is not the time or place to present a wishful thinking forecast.

Q. *How far into the future should an entrepreneur project the numbers?*

A. 3 years
We look the hardest at the first 12 months

Q. *How do you feel about comparing the company to an existing company with vertical, horizontal, competitor and same size and same industry comparisons?*

A. Good to use
We compare a company applying for a loan to a similar company that may already be one of our customers

Q. *An entrepreneur might be going into the business of selling products and find out they are in the business of quick service more than quality of the product. Do you find an entrepreneur may experience a lot of changes in the first year?*

A. Absolutely – 1st 5 years

The first major wall that a company faces after they get out of the starting blocks is when the business achieves 5 million in annual sales. At this point, usually, a new layer of controls becomes necessary along with a beefed-up infrastructure, new policies, procedures, mid-level management, the addition of a CFO, etc.

The owner will usually resist delegation for fear of losing control but the business will likely require some delegation of authority if it is to grow successfully beyond $5MM. The process repeats itself and grows more complicated each time the business doubles it sales (i.e. $10MM, $20MM, etc. Growing a business past certain plateaus is like reinventing the company every couple of years.

Q. *If an entrepreneur does not understand financials do you have a way to help them?*

A. We encourage business owners to get their business advisor involved to coach them, perhaps even suggest they take a basic financial analysis class at a community college. To most entrepreneurs, financial ratios are a foreign language. The banker's job is to educate clients on what certain financial ratios mean and we discuss the importance (to the long-term health of the business) of maintaining certain key ratios.

Q. *What about the executive summary? How long should that be?*

A. 1 page

Q. *How many pages are appropriate for a business plan?*

A. The historical financial statements alone can be upwards of 30 pages if you have multiple years and supporting footnotes. The actual length of the historical financial info section of the plan really depends on how long the company has been in business. In addition, the plan should include bank checking account statements and personal financial statements from the owners. Most business owners submit the above with every loan request but it is not a plan per se.

The narrative portion of the business plan should be around 10 to 20 pages.

Q. *What section do you look at first, second, third?*

A.   1st (Historical financial info). This means the Balance sheet, Income statement, and the owner's personal net worth.

2nd: We drill down and investigate the composition of business and personal assets – real estate is not liquid so while it is good to see, the asset that gives Bank's the greatest sense of comfort is the personal liquidity of the business and or the owner (i.e. cash & marketable security). Personal assets in retirement accounts are only accessible by the owner of the retirement account. They are protected by creditors. We like to see assets that are not shielded from creditors.

3rd The narrative section of the plan.

Q.   *What is the biggest misconception entrepreneurs have when they*
are interviewed by a bank in connection with their loan request?

A.   They think that the banker understands their business as well as they do

They think the banker lends on collateral only and forget that positive cash flow/profits are of even greater importance.

They don't realize bankers need to see a strong primary and a secondary source of repayment.

Loan decisions are largely based on a company's historical accomplishments not on what is projected

Borrower's don't understand how quickly collateral dissipates in a bankruptcy, hence, borrowers think Bankers should lend against inventory and bankers usually discourage inventory financing.

Q.   *How does the loan process differ from how entrepreneurs think it works?*

A.   Entrepreneurs seem to believe there is a faceless loan committee out there somewhere. Usually, there is one key person that calls the shots on a loan. Also, some business owners think a computer makes the decisions. At Endeavor Bank we do not use computers to final loan decisions.

Q. *What happens behind the scenes in the actual loan process?*

A. Historical financial statements are manually entered into a computer spreadsheet program and analyzed. References are checked. Credit reports are studied. The Internet is used to research the industry and learn more about the company. Potential credit structures are discussed along with pricing options to determine what it will take to first and foremost cover the credit risk involved in lending money, the amount needed to cover overhead and to guess what the competition might be proposing.

If a customer seeking a loan tries to "grind" the banks terms, conditions, and pricing to a point that the bank loses interest/incentive to do business with the borrower, the business owner might lose out on an otherwise good banking relationship.

Q. *What is the typical length of time it takes to get a business loan approved and funded?*

A. If a customer comes in with a complete financial package it can take as little as 2 days, however, if the financial package is missing relevant information the loan will be on hold until all of the requested information is forwarded to the bank. The average amount of time to approve and fund a loan is about a week.

Q. *Can you identify an ideal candidate for a loan?*

A. Profitable company
Well-capitalized
Strong reputation
Excellent character
Happy to personally guarantee
Keep a high balance in cash accounts

(Side note: Many Customers feel if they invest their business surplus funds into a sweep account, this money is in the "bank" and hence the banker must, therefore, be enjoying a profitable depository relationship. Truth is the money is in a 3rd party mutual fund company account, and sweep accounts are not typically very beneficial to the bank. Banks can only lend out funds held in core deposit accounts so clients that keep their deposits in the bank are more valuable typically than those that sweep everything out.

Early on in my banking career, I kept calling upon an important customer advising them to invest some of their excess funds into a CD where they would earn some interest income.

This particular client was keeping nearly a million in cash in their non-interest bearing checking account. After months of encouraging the client to invest the funds in an interest-bearing account and hearing the same reply, no thanks, I was surprised when one day the customer came to me and asked me if I thought he was "stupid"

I replied no of course and the client responded that he was indeed quite savvy and had a reason for keeping these funds in an account where he knew he was making the bank a handsome profit.

I soon found out that this client was using this as a tool to make himself so valuable to the bank, that when it came time to call in a favor, the bank asked how high.

The favor came on a Friday evening, before a 3 day weekend when most bankers were ready to head out early. The client needed to borrow $3,000,000 to close a business transaction by Monday morning. Needless to say, I skipped the 3 day weekend and worked non-stop over the weekend, to assure this important client that he would have his loan come Monday. This was no stupid client, he knew exactly what that money in a checking account would buy him, a banker that would say "how high" when he said "jump".

Anything I haven't asked you about that you feel would be good for business owners to know?

Many entrepreneurs try to get off their personal loan guarantee. Such an effort concerns bankers and often the question in my mind is what does the business owner known, that I don't know about their business, that would cause the business owner concern that the loan may not be repaid as expected? For it is only under that scenario that a personal guarantee would ever be drawn upon.

If anyone in your owns a manufacturing company they should consider getting the book, The Goal.

Management bios – past accomplishments are important to us. Always share them with the banker.

More people should go to FDIC.gov and check out the information on banks. They can learn how to find a bank that is most compatible with their business needs and a better fit.

For example we have made more business loans in just the 1 ½ years we've been in business than one of our much larger competitors has done over the last 20 years. To the public, they only know that our competitor is much larger in terms of asset size. What they don't realize, without some due diligence, is that most of our competitor's loans are invested in real estate lending, not business lending. If you go to FDIC.gov you will learn which banks loan to your type of business.

Rather than go to the bank that specializes in real estate lending, they might find it more advantageous to deal with a bank that specializes in business lending, if that is their need.

Also, this website will confirm where a bank is headquartered, their legal lending limit, etc.

Don't forget to interview the banker as well as the bank.

Always interview the banker, not just the bank. Find out:

Does the banker have good knowledge about your business?
Does the banker seem knowledgeable?
Good companies have choices, So remember you are interviewing the bank to see if they are worthy of your business, just as much as the bank is interviewing you to see if you are qualified for the loan that is being requested.

If you were given a choice between selecting to work with an excellent banker (that was employed by a lousy bank) versus working with a lousy banker (who happened to be employed by an excellent bank), go with the excellent banker, and you will be far better off in the long run.

A good banker will overcome the headaches that come with working for a large bureaucratic organization and will work hard for you to be supportive of your banking needs.

Once you find a great banker, invest in the relationship. Stay with your banker, follow them to another bank if they move and solicit your business. Relationships are built with people remember, promises that are kept. A relationship is not with a faceless credit file or a building without a soul. Your relationship with the "banker" is priceless and a good one will take care of you if you perform as agreed.

When interviewing a potential banker to serve you:

Ask;
1. What does your most important client look like?
2. Do I fall into that criteria?
3. If you do fall into the criteria, ask how you can make yourself more important as one of their clients
4. If the answer involves leaving some money on the table as in paying more interest on a loan or keeping more deposits in a checking account (as opposed to sweeping them), ask the bankers what is in it for me, why should I allow you to make more money on our "mutually profitable relationship"? If the banker can't paint a compelling picture, move on.

If you ever have to call a bank for help, make sure you have previously made yourself into a highly valuable, profitable account so that you can be assured that the bank is loyal to you and will jump through hoops to retain your business. Like the example I spoke of previously with the business owner who left a million dollars on deposit in the bank and called in a "mark" when he needed to borrow 3 million, fast, to close a business deal.

Make sure your banker knows you could do something else with your money, you've just chosen to keep it in their bank, make sure they know you are keeping your money with them to maintain a good strong relationship.

23 Investment Banker Tells You How to Get Money from Alternative Financial Sources

760-632-1889
An interview with an
International Investment Banker
Azim Khamisz
7/11/03 updated 10/18/18

What is the difference between an investment banker and a banker?

The main difference between a banker and an investment banker is the banker wants low or no risk loans and tons of personal financials. An investment banker wants to know about the returns and expects more risk and to tolerate that risk they want a higher return.

What is the difference between a venture capitalist and an investment banker?

The main differences between an investment banker and venture capitalist are they may seek an exit quicker, often are more interested in the second round funding. Seek a higher return much more quickly than an investment banker. The venture capitalist is looking for a stronger management team.

How does a business owner find an investment banker?

The best way to find an investment banker is through your advisors

What are some secrets of a loan meeting with an investment banker?

Expect to spend some time getting to know each other. You should check out your investment bankers references and expect they will want to check you out. You will spend a lot of time with each other, it will in both your best interest to check each other out. Expect to pay a monthly retainer and a success fee. The smaller the deal the higher the success fee.

What size companies would be appropriate for seeking help from an investment banker?

Between 2 and 20 million. Your company may have reached a plateau where you need to get to the next level.

How many deals get funded, what are your odds of getting money from an investment banker?
A seasoned investment advisor doesn't accept deals that can't be funded. Azim's success rate is about an 80%

How much should a business owner expect to pay an investment banker for their help?

A business owner will pay a fee for the investment banker to search for money. That amount is similar to the fees for a business advisor or accountant. This fee covers an investment bankers cost. The investment banker starts making a profit when the business gets funded.

How long it will take for a business owner to get money after agreeing to engage the services of an investment advisor?

Four months to a year to get funding through an investment advisor depending on how well the company is prepared.

What is the number one thing an investment banker is looking for?

A business owner must have a business plan for an investment banker to get involved if they don't an investment banker will prepare it with them.

How do you determine how many employees a company should have?

As a rule of thumb, you can divide your revenues by $200,000 and that will tell you how many employees you might have in a typical situation. If your company is generating $1,000,000 in revenue you should have 5 employees.

What is one of the most important measurables an investment banker uses to determine the health of a company?

EBITDA

What is EBITDA?

Earnings before interest, taxes, depreciation, and amortization

An easy way to think about EBITDA is;

If it costs you a dollar to sell a product for a dollar fifty, then your EBITDA is fifty cents.

If it costs you a dollar to sell a product at ninety cents then you have a negative EBITDA of ten cents.

10% of EBITDA on revenues it is not worth as much as a company that has 20%

If a company has $10,000,000 in revenues and an EBITDA of $1,000,000 it won't sell for a lot of money because the EBITDA is only 10% of revenues.

If a company $10,000,000 in revenues and EBITDA of $2,500,000 it will sell for more than a company with 10% EBITDA because the EBITDA is 25%.

Is EBITDA critical for funding through an investment banker?

EBITDA is the determining factor in how much funding an investment banker can raise in capital for growth

How does an investment banker use EBITDA?

EBITDA can be used to analyze the profitability between companies and industries. To determine the value of the company to an investor or buyer. It was originally used to indicate a company's ability to service debt in the 80's. It became popular for companies who had expensive assets that had to be written down over a period of time.

If EBITDA grows over time, it gives investors at least some sense of future potential profitability, which is why some investors look at "EBITDA margin" as a substitute for net margins.

EBITDA can provide a relatively good "apples-to-apples" comparison of a company in an industry to another company in the same industry regardless of size.

For example, EBITDA as a percent of sales (the higher the ratio, the higher the profitability) can be used to find companies that are the most efficient operators in an industry.

The ratio can also be used to evaluate different industry trends over time. Because it removes the impact of financing large capital investments and depreciation from the analysis, EBITDA can be used to compare the profitability trends of, say, "heavy" industries (like automobile manufacturers) to hi-tech companies.

A simple explanation of EBITDA
by
James Wittmack

Say you're six years old and want to open a lemonade stand, hoping **Coca-Cola** (NYSE: KO) will eventually figure out a way to buy your operation. You have no money, so mom and dad front the capital equipment costs: $30 for lemonade, cups, sugar, water, and signage.

At the end of the day, mom and dad want to know how much money you made. They don't want a figure that's been adjusted for interest payments on the debt you owe them, taxes, and depreciation of the fixed assets. That's the idea behind EBITDA, to give investors a sense of how much money a young or fast-growing company is generating before it pays it all out to creditors, IRS, etc...

EBITDA is …..Earnings before interest, taxes, depreciation, and amortization

Taxes are

A levy placed on the profit of a firm; different rates are used for different levels of profits

Depreciation is

An expense recorded to reduce the value of a long-term tangible asset. Since it is a non-cash expense, it increases free cash flow while decreasing the amount of a company's reported earnings

Amortization is

The paying off of debt in regular installments over a period of time.

The deduction of capital expenses over a specific period of time. Similar to depreciation, it is a method of measuring the "consumption" of the value of long-term assets like equipment or buildings.

24 ADDITIONAL RESOURCES AND READING FOR HELP

Additional Resources and Reading That You May Find Helpful

Type the following in a search engine; "how do I find a bank that loans to my type of business in the location your business is in".

CDC small business finance is a not-for-profit lender that provides low-interest, affordable financing to small businesses so they can expand, grow and create jobs throughout California, Arizona and Nevada. The company specializes in SMA lending, including the SBA-504 loan for purchasing commercial/industrial buildings. CDC also offers the community advantage loan for up to $250,000 for working capital, equipment, inventory, tenant improvements and business acquisition. Additionally, CDC offers the SBA microloan for up to $50,000. In 40 years, CDC has provided nearly $18 billion in capital to more than 11,000 growing small businesses, particularly minority - and women - owned companies. Through small business expansion, CDC has been a catalyst for the creation of over 300,000 jobs.

GETTING THE MONEY OVER THE FENCE

800.611.5170 AND WEBSITE - WWW.CDCLOANS.COM

The Harvard Business Review Paperback Series
Harvard Business Review on MANAGING PEOPLE. Harvard Business School Publishing, Boston, MA 02163, 1999

Ries, Al. FOCUS. HarperCollins Publishers, Inc., 1997

Beckwith, Harry. The Invisible Touch. Warner Books, Inc., 2000

Hammon, John s., Keeney, Ralph L., Raiffa, Howard. Smart Choices. Harvard Business School Press, 1999

Thielen, David. The 12 Simple Secrets of Microsoft Management. McGraw-Hill, Inc., 1999

Slater, Robert. Jack Welch and the GE Way. McGraw-Hill Companies, Inc. 1999

Goleman, Daniel. Working with Emotional Intelligence. Bantam Doubleday Dell Publishing Group, Inc., 1998

O'Connor, Ph.D., Michael J., Alessandra, Tony. The Platinum Rule. Warner Books, 1996

Watkins, Michael, Ciampa, Dan. Right from the Start. Harvard Business School Press, 1999

Smart, Ph.D., Bradford D. Topgrading. Prentice Hall, Inc., 1999

Wittmack, James. S.. Where is your business going?
How to craft a road map to win the game of business
Self Published 2003 minddumpinc.com

Wittmack, James S. What does it take to SUCCEED in business?
Will your company be one of the 2.5% that is still in business after 10 years?
2003 minddumpinc.com
Wittmack, James S. Lessons learned from having my business stolen at gunpoint.
Mission Critical solutions you must know to avoid bad surprises
2018 minddumpinc.com

ABOUT THE AUTHOR

GETTING THE MONEY OVER THE FENCE

James S. Wittmack had his business stolen from him at gunpoint in 1989. Since then he has been doing everything he can to prevent business owners from ever getting into a similar predicament. That's why he developed his proprietary process he calls "MIND DUMP".

MIND DUMP is a 5 phase 3 hour to 4 day in-depth, inspirational process that liberates fresh thinking so you can change the world.

"MIND DUMP" allows business owners to "get out of their head" and clearly understand their business issues, eliminating problems until they are literally. Participants receive a comprehensive strategy for success and optional accountability meetings to keep them on track.
A Master Strategist can identify complex dynamic patterns others don't comprehend and implement a hybrid of options when options are limited. A master strategist is one of an elite group who set the regulations, standards, and ideals. Regarded by experts as being "the" expert.

Why is a Master Strategist with 40 plus years experience better for you than 20 people with ten years experience equaling 200 years experience?

Suppose you have a problem stemming from a 30-year-old technology that was discontinued 20 years ago. 20 people with ten years experience seek the advice of a Master Strategist, and so should you.

As a child, James dreamed of being the most successful CEO in the world. His perspective changed during a semester abroad as part of World Campus Afloat through Chapman College. After spending time with tribespeople who had next to nothing, including no education or electricity, but were very happy, he realized having much money has little to do with happiness and success.

Following college, James worked as a turnaround expert and troubleshooter in retail and distribution for 12 years. For the next eight years, he owned a furniture manufacturing company that he built from scratch into a globally recognized brand. Manufacturing custom furniture sold through design centers for large homes and hotel lobbies. James Mexican partner stole his company from him at gunpoint. Reflecting on what happened, driving back across the border he realized he could have prevented this if he had access to quick answers to mission-critical issues.

That's when he developed the proprietary process he calls "MIND DUMP." J.I.T.S. - Just in time strategies to cope with rapid change. His focus is to do everything he can to prevent any business owner from getting into a similar predicament. MIND DUMP allows business owners to get "out of their head" and clearly understand their business issues. Business owners achieve targeted outcomes with dramatic financial results in an accelerated timeline. Within 3 hours to 4 days problems are eliminated.

He gained in-depth knowledge and strategic expertise as an investment advisor for nine years with American Express Financial Advisors / NY Life. A struggling high-end furniture manufacture firm recruited him to turn the company around as the CEO. After a successful turnaround, James served as an advisor for national management consulting companies out of Chicago and Dallas.

www.ingramcontent.com/pod-product-compliance
Lightning Source LLC
Chambersburg PA
CBHW020435220526
45464CB00002B/720